MONEY, COLOR AND SEX IN HAWAI'I POLITICS

Library of Congress Catalog Card
Number: 98-67131

First Printing, August 1998
1 2 3 4 5 6 7 8 9

ISBN 1-56647-218-0

Design by Jane Hopkins
Illustrations by John Pritchett

Mutual Publishing
1215 Center Street, Suite 210
Honolulu, Hawaii 96816
Telephone (808) 732-1709
Fax (808) 734-4094
e-mail: mutual@lava.net

Printed in Australia

MONEY, COLOR AND SEX IN HAWAI'I POLITICS

Chad Blair

MUTUAL PUBLISHING

TABLE OF CONTENTS

ACKNOWLEDGMENTS

For their assistance in the researching and writing of this book, my thanks to Darren Akau, Dean Alegado, Amy Agbayani, David Bertelson, Dan Boylan, Jerry Burris, Meda Chesney-Lind, Jon Ciliberto, Tom Coffman, Bill Daly, Sandra Enoki, Mayumi Fukumoto, Mary George, Glen Grant, Colleen Gouveia, David Hagino, Mazie Hirono, Harold Higashi, Arnold Hiura, Paul Hooper, Judith Hughes, Henry Iwasa, Wendy Kaleiwahea, Franklin Kometani, Ian Lind, Lowell Kurashige, Calvin Leong, Jack Lewin, James McCutcheon, Martha Ross, Franklin Odo, Dennis Ogawa, Edgar Porter, Richard Rapson, Paul Rausch, Robert Rees, Randall Roth, Pat Saiki, Stan Saiki Jr., Robert Schmitt, A. A. Smyser, Leslie Stewart, Monica Stitt-Bergh, Charles Toguchi, Rick Trimillos, Dan Tuttle, Geraldine Uyeuten, Bob Wernet and Jackie Young.

My special thanks to my family and to Donnë Florence, who edited the manuscript and provided wise counsel throughout the research and writing of this book.

"A Special Place"

MONEY, COLOR AND SEX are excellent lenses through which to examine Hawai'i politics. They refer to class, race or ethnicity and gender and sexual orientation—in other words, the fundamental characteristics of all people. These characteristics greatly influence beliefs and behaviors that extend over generations. Their relation to political participation is critical, for it is in the political arena that a society's ability to uphold democratic principles can best be judged. In choosing those who lead us, and rejecting those we do not want, we say a great deal about ourselves. As this book shows, what the people of Hawai'i have said is as promising as it is troubling.

Hawai'i's promise attracts the attention of many. Shortly after the United States congressional election in November 1994, a nationally-known political reporter and a biographer of former President Ronald Reagan flew to Hawai'i for a visit. Lou Cannon had been invited to be on a Honolulu panel addressing the media and government, but he was also looking for fresh insight into the recent election, for it appeared voters nationwide had launched a conservative tidal wave. Led by soon-to-be House Speaker Newt Gingrich and a host of newly elected Republican representatives waving their "Contract With America"—a ten-point legislative manifesto that included term-limit proposals and a balanced-budget amendment—historic change was in the air. Media commentators heralded the election as the beginning of a new era. Bill Clinton, the Democratic president, appeared weakened; his election two years earlier had itself seemed to launch a new era, one that included more women, gays and minorities in government. Clinton had even appointed a cabinet that "looked like America," rather than yet another group of wealthy, white males.

By 1996, however, the conservative tide had washed out. Much of the "Contract" had not been honored, and Gingrich's ratings were abysmal. Borrowing Republican ideas and moving toward the political center, Clinton was reelected to the White House in 1996, but Republicans kept their majority in Congress and state governorships. Some observers called it "gridlock," while others said another wave of change would surely follow. Longtime political observers like Cannon knew it for what it was, though: the continuous ebb and flow of two-party politics in a representative democracy.

Some 2,400 miles west of the U.S. mainland, something very different happened in November 1994: nothing at all. The tropical islands where surfing originated had caught no wave. Rather, a Democratic lieutenant governor succeeded a Democratic governor, as had happened without interruption for over three decades. The state Legislature remained solidly in Democrats' hands, as did the state's congressional delegation. While the rest of America experienced dramatic political change, Hawai'i voters woke up the morning of November 9, 1994, to embrace the same political leadership as the day before. The occasion was hailed by power brokers of the islands' status quo—Democrats, labor unions, members of some ethnic groups—and bemoaned by perennial outsiders—Republicans, small business owners, members of other groups.

Cannon was fascinated by Hawai'i's political stability, particularly in light of the recent passing of Proposition 187 in his and Reagan's home state. "While California was rising up in wrath against its multi-ethnic future by passing a demagogic anti-immigration initiative, this peaceful outpost of democracy was reaffirming its melting-pot destiny by electing Ben Cayetano as governor," he wrote. "Hawai'i...has set a tone for the modern, multiracial progressive state." Cannon believed one of America's smallest states might well serve as a model for one of its largest; in the early part of the next century, after all, California will likely become the first mainland state where no racial or ethnic group is a majority.

Cannon's sentiments were echoed locally. *Honolulu Weekly* political columnist Robert M. Rees, noting the mainland's ideological shift, praised Hawai'i for retaining its political tradition by reelecting its liberal representatives. "I believe we ought to remain as we are," he wrote, "an outpost of tolerance." Others noted that no American state was as egalitarian in political representation as Hawai'i. After attending Ben Cayetano's 1994 inauguration, local political commentator Dan Boylan wrote in O'ahu's *MidWeek*: "The son of an immigrant Filipino who spent his life working in a rich white men's club in Waikīkī, was being sworn in as governor on the 'Iolani Palace bandstand. With the daughter of a Japanese immigrant beside him as his lieutenant governor [Mazie Hirono], he replaced the son of rural Hawaiian ranchers, John Waihee. And he was sworn in by the son of Korean immigrants, [Hawai'i's Chief Justice] Ronald Moon. To reach his spot on the bandstand, Cayetano defeated a son of Italian immigrants to the United States, Frank Fasi, and the daughter of Japanese immigrants, Pat Saiki. The racial inclusion represented on the 'Iolani bandstand this past inaugural day, of men and women named Waihee and Cayetano and Hirono and Moon, is Hawai'i's greatness. It distinguishes us from any other society in the world."

On the surface, Hawai'i's 1994 gubernatorial election did indeed seem to confirm the long-common description of Hawai'i as a model for diverse communities. America's first and only governor of Hawaiian ancestry, Democrat John Waihee, ineligible by law to run for a third term, was succeeded by his lieutenant governor, Ben Cayetano. Cayetano's election as the nation's first and only governor of Filipino ancestry illustrated for many the continuation of a pattern of power sharing among Hawai'i's largest ethnic groups—Europeans, Japanese, Filipinos and Hawaiians (most island residents usually do not add "American" when stating their ethnicity, a custom that emphasizes their ethnic origins). Waihee had succeeded three-term Democrat George Ariyoshi, the nation's first and only governor of Japanese ancestry; Ariyoshi had succeeded three-term Democrat John Burns, a Caucasian.

Listing the state's governors, however, does not fully illustrate the state's diverse political tapestry, for the entire slate of '94 candidates reflected a multicultural mix unparalleled anywhere else in the U.S. Taken together, all 35 candidates for the state's highest offices that year were a cross section of Hawai'i's people—members of most ethnic groups, men and women, young and old, island-born residents and transplanted mainlanders, and the rich, poor and most classes in between. Diversity was not limited to Hawai'i's gubernatorial election. A special nonpartisan election for Honolulu mayor included among the prime contenders two white males, one Japanese-American female and a male of Asian and Pacific Island ancestry. Another Japanese-American woman and white male were reelected to the U.S. House, while a Hawaiian-Chinese male was reelected to the U.S. Senate. Lastly, campaigns for Honolulu City Council, mayoral and council races for Hawai'i, Maui and Kaua'i counties, and state Legislature elections featured men and women of various political affiliations, ethnic backgrounds and sexual orientation.

Such evidence might lead an observer to conclude that Hawai'i is the one state where America's political ideals are made manifest. Perhaps that was what George Ariyoshi had in mind when he declared during his gubernatorial campaigns that Hawaiʻi was "a special place." But Hawaiʻi's apparently unique niche masks a political structure that rewards some groups at the expense of others. Hawaiʻi is indeed "special," but not in the manner many have been led to believe.

The year 1994 was not unique; the candidates for nearly every election in post-statehood Hawaiʻi are similarly diverse. But the fact that politicians in Hawaiʻi hail from backgrounds more mixed than in any other American state does *not* mean Hawaiʻi has transcended class, race and gender divisions. In fact, politics in these islands are quite exclusive: no ethnic group dominates local politics, yet some groups have much more influence than others. Wealth and power are mainly shared by members of some groups, while others are mired in low-income, low-status jobs. Sex and sexual orientation stratify Hawaiʻi, too. Many of the cultures represented locally favor men over women. Though the state has produced several noteworthy female politicians and women have moved increasingly into the mainstream work force and positions of authority, most Hawaiʻi elected officials have been male, including those who have held the state's highest offices. Hawaiʻi is perceived by some as relatively free of discrimination against homosexuals, partly because some island cultures, especially Native Hawaiians, openly accept their gay and lesbian members. Nevertheless, a majority of residents and their lawmakers choose to deny homosexuals the same rights as heterosexuals.

Hawaiʻi—the most geographically isolated land mass anywhere—leads efforts to achieve peaceful coexistence and prosperity among diverse peoples, but no one should think those efforts are complete or that they can be declared successful. In fact, Hawaiʻi is a progressive, cosmopolitan American society with critical problems and great inequalities— as well as alarming signs that these matters are worsening. But there is also great promise that Hawaiʻi might still represent something that humankind may aspire to. Its experiment with representative democracy among diverse peoples might yet serve as instruction to America and the world, showing what it has done right, as well as what it could do better.

Multicultural Politics

Hawai'i's modern political history begins with Western contact in the late 1700s and continues through the Hawaiian monarchy period of the last century, its overthrow in 1893 by white-American-male-business interests, U.S. annexation five years later, territorial rule under Republicans until the middle 1950s and Democrat control since statehood in 1959. A sugar and pineapple plantation system fueled the economy during much of this time. Its development was also the primary reason whites usurped Hawaiian authority and imported foreign workers who created a multicultural society. Though the plantation-based economy is gone, the plantations' social, political and economic consequences remain, particularly evident in the rise of organized labor that developed as a result of plantation conditions and led to the gradual decline of the so-called "Big Five" plantation companies. Tourism now drives the state's economy, and local residents are as beholden to its power as they once were to the plantations.

These consequences are this book's central focus, for they powerfully dictate Hawai'i's politics in specific ways: those elected to office in Hawai'i over the past half-century have almost all belonged to the Democratic party and share similar backgrounds; they are largely from the upper classes; they are predominantly white and Japanese American; and there are *far* more males than females in office.

The people and history of Hawai'i are unique in others ways, however. The islands, like the mainland, have indigenous people, but Native Hawaiians and American Indians are different. For one thing, Hawaiians total one-fifth of Hawai'i's population and significantly influence local politics. Some mainland states have ethnically diverse populations, but only

California comes close to Hawai'i's multicultural milieu. For over 200 years no state but Hawai'i had elected an Asian American or Pacific Islander as its governor (in 1996, Washington elected a Chinese-American governor). Hawai'i is the only state that does not have a white majority. Lastly, while Hawai'i shares an agricultural background with much of the mainland, only the South had an experience comparable to Hawai'i's plantation system. Just as the consequences of slavery can still be seen in the South and elsewhere in the U.S. as blacks struggle for equality with whites, Hawai'i's plantation system created the split society of modern Hawai'i that benefits some but not others.

However, as on the mainland, Hawai'i and its people are changing. The state's population is significantly different from what it was only a decade ago, and considerably different from the time of statehood. Some ethnic group numbers and their influence have increased, others have decreased and new groups have arrived to compete with old ones. High intermarriage rates have produced individuals who often have no particular ethnic identity—or several. Wealth, while still concentrated among certain groups, has been affected by a lengthy statewide economic downturn at the twentieth century's close. Some observers have insisted that Hawai'i is becoming a home to only the rich and the poor, with the large middle classes in between forced to seek their livelihood elsewhere. Though women struggle for parity with men, women are now serious candidates for all state, city and county offices. The issue of same-sex marriage, at the forefront of legislative and judicial concerns in recent years, has forced the state's people to deal with other aspects of civil and equal rights. Finally, Hawaiian sovereignty, a serious issue with repercussions for the entire state, will likely emerge in the twenty-first century as the islands' greatest social, political and economic challenge.

The Gathering Place

The following chapters explore characteristics of Hawai'i's people and politics, including how money, color and sex influence one another; the wealth and population patterns among Hawai'i's peoples; the strength of their ethnic identities; their voting behavior and political participation; and attitudes and tendencies about relationships to power. The island of O'ahu and, to a lesser extent, the island county of Hawai'i are the focus of the book, for the two islands together have 85 percent of the state's population. O'ahu has about three-fourths of the state's people, or 840,000. This figure includes military personnel stationed or home-ported on O'ahu. With tourists and transient military personnel, the state population increases to over 1.2 million, according to the 1990 Census, though state Department of Health surveys indicate that military personnel and their dependents number less than 100,000.

Hawai'i has only two levels of government—state and county— though, because of its size and power, Honolulu is essentially a third level between the other two. Though it is geographically the smallest of Hawai'i's four island counties, the City & County of Honolulu is the center of business and government for Hawai'i. Appropriately, O'ahu is known locally as "the gathering place." Honolulu's two daily newspapers include coverage of all islands and are circulated throughout the state, and its commercial television stations and the state's public television station are broadcast statewide via satellite. (The island counties of Hawai'i, Maui and Kaua'i also have their own newspapers, radio stations and cable outlets.) Some have argued that Honolulu's county's official name should be changed to "O'ahu County" to more accurately reflect geographical reality rather than to continue distinguishing the state's Capitol at the expense of the island.

A city of just under half a million people, Honolulu is the home of most major candidates for governor and lieutenant governor. In the state's 40-year history, only two politicians who have held statewide office hailed from outside O'ahu—

lieutenant governors Nelson Doi (1974-78) and Jimmy Kealoha (1959-62), both from the island of Hawai'i. Called the "Big Island," Hawai'i is twice the combined geographical size of all the other islands in the state and has the second largest population at 130,500. The state's congressional delegation also calls Honolulu home (although most of the legislators' time is spent 5,000 miles away in the nation's capital), except for the 2nd District seat, which represents all of the state outside urban Honolulu. This seat has been held for most of its existence by Maui native Patsy Mink. Maui is the third largest island in population, with 109,000, and the county includes the islands of Moloka'i and Lāna'i, as well as Maui. The islands of Hawai'i, Maui, Kaua'i, Moloka'i and Lāna'i are often referred to as the "outer" or "neighbor" islands by O'ahu residents, illustrating an O'ahu- or Honolulu-centric bias. A seventh main island, Ni'ihau, is privately owned by the Robinson family (they are white) and has some 200 residents of mostly Hawaiian ancestry. The Big Island, Maui and Kaua'i each has its own dynamic political histories that are distinct from O'ahu's and worthy of examination. But Honolulu is the political and population center of the state, and so its people and politics are the central focus of this book.

Explaining Hawai'i

The material for this book is drawn from a variety of sources, for there are many books and articles about Hawai'i's social, political and economic history. The intention here is not to repeat what has already been said, but instead to interpret material in a fresh way—to *synthesize* what has been said and done—to reveal basic characteristics of local politics. Many island residents know very little about their own social and political histories, and even less about what scholars, journalists and politicians have said and written about them. Many of the more useful and important views are collected here. Though they are as complementary as they are contradictory, the authors of all these views share one common goal: to help explain the people and politics of Hawai'i.

The next three chapters look at the role of *money, color* and *sex* in Hawai'i's politics, respectively, but the material often overlaps. The chapter titled "Money: 'Vote Dem, Save Job'" looks at observations and events concerning *class* in Hawai'i. It includes a brief account of the social and economic history of Hawai'i since 1778, particularly the development of the plantation system; the rise of unions and their membership; the relationships of agricultural, military, tourism and union interests to Hawai'i's political parties; a brief look at the state's economy in the 1990s; a look at centers of political power in the islands; and the influence of class on local elections.

"Color: 'Look for the Skin'" deals with *race* and *ethnicity*. The chapter examines Hawai'i's ethnic groups; includes profiles of whites, Japanese, Hawaiians and Filipinos, as well as Chinese, who rank fifth in overall population numbers but hold considerable influence; and briefly illustrates the voting behavior and political participation of these groups. The chapter continues with a look at "local identity," considers the impact of intermarriage among Hawai'i's populations, and details a history of the role of race in local politics.

"Sex: 'Three Steps Behind'" looks at gender, sexual orientation and sex roles in Hawai'i. It includes the labor history of women, their status compared with men and attitudes toward sex and power. It also considers the political participation of women in Hawai'i—in particular white, Asian and Polynesian women—and includes profiles of recent elections and candidates.

Lastly, "The Promise of Hawai'i" considers the effectiveness of representative democracy in multicultural Hawai'i as its people and politics enter a new century. If Hawai'i has outperformed other states in the pursuit of a democratic ideal, it still has some distance to go in achieving that ideal. Still, its past demonstrates that Hawai'i's people have the political will and resources to fulfill its great promise.

Money: "Vote Dem, Save Job"

"He or she who has vast sums of money is a viable and probably winning candidate," *MidWeek* political columnist Dan Boylan has observed. "He or she who does not—no matter how intelligent, imaginative and virtuous— is not. Welcome once again to America's patented cash-register democracy."

Boylan is not wrong about that, but the role of money in Hawai'i elections is also more complex than he suggests. No political party in any other American city or state has held power as long—half a century—and as exclusively as Democrats in Hawai'i. Their record is bested only by Hawai'i Republicans, in power from 1898 to 1954. The 1954 turnaround—some have called it Hawai'i's second revolution—owed as much to myths about money, power and socioeconomic class as it did to the actual dollars Democratic candidates had at their disposal.

Since 1962, when they captured the governor's office, Hawai'i Democrats have owned the myth—the popular belief that Republicans are the party of the wealthy, Democrats the party of working people. They have made the myth a powerful political weapon, even as they improved their own financial reality, laying claim to the resources of Hawai'i's labor unions and other moneyed interests. Actually having the money to conduct successful campaigns, and the power to dispense favors that comes with election victories, has unquestionably helped keep Hawai'i Democrats in office. The greater mystery is how—with all that money and power—the party has managed to retain its popular image as the champion of the underdog.

Like many tenacious myths, this one has its roots in historical fact. When whites settled in Hawai'i in the ninteteenth century, they abolished Hawaiian social structures and established Western customs in their place. Hawaiians lost their language, their culture, their very way of life, and adopted—not necessarily by choice, nor uniformly—Christian religions, the English language, Western habits and the American concept of land ownership. The Great Mahele (*mahele* is Hawaiian for "division"), a plan agreed upon in 1848 by the Hawaiian monarchy and influential non-Hawaiian residents, led to the purchase of lands by non-Hawaiians, many of whom would use these lands for commercial purposes. This marked the beginning of the Hawaiian plantation system. It made some whites and Hawaiians wealthy and unintentionally made possible the multiethnic culture that exists today, but it was an oppressive, segregated operation. Many Hawaiians and whites elected not to work in the sugar cane and, later, pineapple fields, so inexpensive laborers were imported, mostly from Asia. Unfortunately, it was the sad pattern for each immigrant group to experience oppression from those who had arrived earlier and in turn to oppress groups that followed, in a pattern similar to U.S. mainland immigrant patterns. This cycle of oppression was tacitly encouraged by the white plantation owners, collectively known as the "Big Five": Alexander & Baldwin, Castle & Cooke, Theo H. Davies & Co., C. Brewer & Co., and American Factors, or Amfac.

The segregated system established by plantation owners effectively determined the life path for each ethnic group in Hawai'i, and thus its future standing. As Lawrence W. Fuchs explained in a well-known passage from *Hawaii Pono*: "For the kamaaina haoles [local-born whites] the goal was to control; for the Hawaiians, to recapture the past; for the Portuguese, to be considered haole; for the Chinese, to win economic independence; for the Japanese, to be accepted; for the Filipinos, to return to their home in the Philippines." Fuchs published his study of Hawai'i in 1961, and his work chronicles the direction of each ethnic group up to the time of statehood in 1959. While the goals of ethnic groups have changed, and generalizations about ethnic groups in modern Hawai'i are loaded with stereotypes and errors—for example, Portuguese are considered white by census takers, and most Filipinos in Hawai'i likely do *not* want to return to the Philippines—the socioeconomic destiny of Hawai'i's peoples is still determined by the old plantation divisions, and it is almost impossible to separate issues of ethnicity from the discussion of socioeconomic class.

From Plantations to Unions

Wayne S. Wooden explained in *What Price Paradise?* that a two-class system existed during the plantation period—whites maintained economic control, and mostly nonwhite workers did the hard labor. This system was not rigid, and some members of the laboring groups were able to achieve upward mobility once they moved off the plantations. This was especially true of the Chinese, who were the first immigrant group to work the plantations, the group that stayed there the shortest time, and the first group to leave. There was no middle class in plantation-era Hawai'i, Wooden explained. Each ethnic group had in common its own experiences and shared obligations toward the group. While they had obvious differences, they also shared a sense of community—an experience which generally excluded the *kama'āina* elite.

Whites did share an alliance with the Hawaiian royalty, however, which served to separate these two groups (especially whites) from other, mostly immigrant Asian groups. This policy of division kept racial tensions at a minimum. Separate school systems, neighborhoods and other social institutions further separated whites from the laboring nonwhites.

With the Great Depression in the 1930s, World War II in the 1940s, the rise of the Democratic Party and unions in the 1950s and the plantation systems that were gradually replaced by service-industry jobs in the 1960s, a middle class began to emerge in Hawai'i. The period after statehood was marked by a five-class society, according to Wooden. Wooden's categories revealed the strong connection between *money* and *color*. It's possible to divide almost any society into any number of socioeconomic classes, of course. What makes Hawai'i's classes seem different from other U.S. states is that the most economically powerful class (or classes) is *not* almost exclusively white. As Richard L. Rapson wrote in *Fairly Lucky You Live Hawaii!*: "The statistics suggest that Hawaii verges on being a two-class society, divided between Orientals and Caucasians at the top and Polynesians, Filipinos, and mixed groups at the bottom. The affluent groups share neighborhoods, schools, and certain attitudes with one another which may separate them from the less affluent."

Plantation labor uprisings began in the late-1800s, but most were quickly stamped out by planters. In the early decades of the twentieth century, plantation workers could be brought together over a particular cause, but once the immediate problem was settled, unity disappeared. "The effectiveness of labor organizations was diminished by the fact that they [the workers] were unified more by race than by cause," Edward Joesting explains in *Hawaii: An Uncommon History*.

But things changed dramatically after World War I. When primarily Japanese and Filipino workers organized and went on strike to protest wages and conditions, they began to think of themselves less as men and women of different nationalities and more as members of a working class. A major plantation strike in 1920 in particular raised that consciousness. The Japanese were the first ethnic group to organize a labor union and the first to organize a major sugar strike for higher wages, but theirs were small protests that did not get the attention of the sugar planters. It was only by combining forces with Filipino workers that the Japanese workers could organize effectively to ask for higher wages and other demands.

By the late 1930s, collective bargaining between unions and employers had begun. Hawai'i's most successful and militant union, the International Longshoremen's and Warehousemen's Union (ILWU), soon took form. By 1941, the ILWU had organized dock workers in both Hawai'i and San Francisco and controlled the flow of goods to and from Hawai'i. World War II and martial law halted most union activity, but planning for the future continued. The ILWU, with the help of mainland labor leader Jack Hall, began to organize not only longshoremen, but also the sugar and pineapple workers. In 1946, it led 21,000 workers on 33 plantations to leave their jobs, the largest labor strike in Hawai'i's history up to that time. The planters gave in to most of the ILWU demands, and a new, powerful force in Hawai'i's politics emerged.

Along with the rise in union power came the rise of the Democratic Party, which had functioned for half a century in the shadow of Republican rule. "During those years the Democratic party had one common, unifying objective," according to Joesting. "It wanted to overthrow the existing power structure—and that meant the Republicans." This unifying objective brought together diverse segments of the Democratic party, including the radical ILWU on the one end and conservatives on the other. Both groups would lose to those who occupied the middle ground. Even moderate Democrats were still too radical for Republicans in 1954—the Republicans attempted but failed to portray them as

Communists. But that year, for the first time in Hawaiian history, Democrats gained control of both houses of the territorial Legislature. Nearly a half-century later, the Democrats still have legislative control.

Political change did not immediately bring social or economic change. Class separation along racial lines continued, but the racial divisions fostered on the plantations were giving way to the collective power that unionization promised. Though plantation laborers had been transformed into a stable, better-paid class of skilled workers, the only employment opportunities besides agriculture were in the secondary market of "dead-end, low-paid, casual labor. The major unions in construction and the service industry have long recognized that if the local people were to prosper in Hawaii, there would have to be a considerable expansion of employment," Edward D. Beechert writes in *Hawaii: An Uncommon History*.

The unions had succeeded in organizing workers, but they had a greater problem to face—namely, what to do with a steadily growing populace that needed work. Unions accordingly endorsed the Democratic Party's program of economic development in the 1950s and 1960s, and the union-Democratic Party relationship has continued to the present day. But that relationship can no longer ensure prosperity for many of its supporters. Hawai'i's economic development boom peaked by the 1970s; after a brief burst of growth in the late 1980s, the economy entered a deep trough in the 1990s from which it is not likely to emerge easily or soon. Agricultural employment, meanwhile, has sharply declined over the past few decades, reflecting changes that had been in the making for half a century. Job shifts related to these changes have brought new challenges to the efforts of unions and workers, for the jobs that remained were mostly in the service industry. "Hawaii, like the United States, was moving toward a structure of employment ever more dominated by jobs that were poorly paid, unchanging, and unproductive," says Beechert. "That the unions have not been as successful in altering these conditions in the tourist industry as they were in the basic industries of Hawaii suggests only that the character of the opposition has changed."

Authors David McClain, Robert M. Rees and Charles H. Turner argue that unions are still effective, but, because they have become so much a part of the establishment, they have lost the passion that got them organized in the first place and now ironically stand in the way of progress. Union membership still remains at about 30 percent of all island workers (nearly twice as high as mainland union membership). Some union membership even increased in recent years. According to the state's Department of Business, Economic Development and Tourism (DBEDT), union membership in the 1990s was about 165,000, or just under 15 percent of the state population. In the public sector—meaning federal, state and county workers— almost 60 percent of employees are union members, compared to less than one-fourth of the private sector work force. Union presence in government is distributed among several unions, including the Hawaii Government Employees Association (HGEA), the Hawaii State Teachers Association (HSTA), the University of Hawaii Professional Assembly (UHPA) and the United Public Workers (UPW). The State of Hawaii Organization of Police Officers (SHOPO) and the Hawaii Fire Fighters Association (HFFA) are also powerful unions of note.

McClain and his co-authors argue that the unions protect the interests of workers in the hotel and related industries, but in government they have succumbed to the tendency of bureaucracies toward "survival and self-aggrandizement." Their relationship with the Democratic Party works to maintain the status quo. "The government unions prosper, the politicians get reelected, and it's all paid for by the taxpayers," they wrote.

"Today's unions look only slightly like the unions of statehood," explains *Hawaii Business* reporter Jeff Barrus. "On the whole, labor now has fatter wallets, whiter collars and less red in the ranks." Labor's influence has declined since the 1950s, mainly because of the phase-out of sugar production and the rise of government unionism, but it still remains a potent political force. The HGEA, the UPW, the HSTA, the UHPA, the SHOPO and the HFFA all developed in the 1970s, reflecting the rise of the public sector as a whole. Today's unions are better financed than their predecessors, and each has a political action committee. They have moved politically from the left to the center. Their members are also from diverse professions and socioeconomic classes who tend to vote more as individuals and less along union lines.

Though they represent almost one-third of the state's work force, unions can no longer guarantee that they will "get out the vote." However, union support is still in demand— particularly government unions—and union influence is not expected to decrease any time soon. "Since labor stood up to management in the late 1950s, since it helped elect Jack Burns in 1962, it has gotten its candidate into the governor's mansion with regularity every four years," Barrus notes. So closely connected are unions and the state government that Governor Ben Cayetano ordered state flags to fly at half-staff following the death in 1997 of longtime labor leader Art Rutledge, father of Teamsters head Tony Rutledge.

Democrats vs. Republicans

Central to the power of unions in Hawai'i is their collaboration with the Democratic Party, and each has insured the other's survival. Nevertheless, it is a mistake to attribute the Democrats' continuing strength entirely to labor unions. As George Cooper and Gavan Daws explained in *Land and Power in Hawaii*, close association between island businesses— especially land developers, their investors and their lawyers— and elected Democratic officials swelled the coffers of not a few local Democrats in the 1960s and 1970s.

Still, perceptions of clear class differences between the parties are pervasive, and they are used to great effect in local political campaigns. Many island voters believe that there is historical justification for keeping modern Hawai'i politics in the hands of Democrats. The Republican Party that controlled Hawai'i for the first half of the twentieth century was "a white man's party," a fact understood even by Hawaiians who voted Republican, explained Gavan Daws in *Shoal of Time*. The Democrats' only hope was the anonymity of the voting booth. "Over the years a sturdy folklore, based on fact, sprang up about managers who planted political spies among their workers, or who watched the movement of the string attached to the pencil in the voting booth, and then held the marked ballot up to the light before dropping it in the ballot box," he wrote. It was apparent to the Democrats that the only way to defeat this white exclusiveness was to be racially *inclusive* themselves. It was the ILWU in the 1940s and 1950s, under the command of Jack Hall (who was white), that first forced this issue. Later, the Republican establishment would be shaken not only by labor interests but by liberals in the public school system and at the University of Hawai'i, political opportunists with no connections to the Republicans, a few radicals, disaffected Hawaiian and part-Hawaiian patronage seekers, small business owners and professionals (mostly white or Asian) who operated on the edges of the Big Five domain, and—most critically—young Japanese-American veterans of World War II who got their education with the help of the G.I. Bill. Thus, the Democrats' racial inclusiveness won them a wider spectrum of socioeconomic classes.

When the Democrats finally won control of the territorial Legislature in 1954, however, the opposite political mood prevailed on the mainland, which was largely in Republican hands. Similarly, Hawai'i had been under the control of Republicans during Democrat Franklin D. Roosevelt's long presidency. It has often been the pattern for Hawai'i to be at political odds with the mainland, a matter some point to with pride, while others lament that the islands are out of step with national trends. In terms of political participation, however, Hawai'i is very much in line with mainland patterns, particularly in perception of party interests and membership. Some 30 years ago, UH scholar Norman Meller profiled island party politics: "In Hawaii, the Democratic Party in the past has tended to attract the support of the poorer classes.... The leadership of the Republican Party was merely another manifestation in different guise of the same group which enjoyed economic and social dominance in the community.... This, of course, tended to have ethnic overtones, as Orientals comprised a larger proportion of the lower socioeconomic segments of the Island community." Thus, the Republican Party in Hawai'i has been seen as the party of big business and whites, while the Democratic Party is that of the "little people" (or nonwhites and/or the working class).

Such perceptions play no small part in most elections, especially in Democratic campaigns. "Many of the events in Hawaii's recent history are surrounded by myth," wrote Paul C. Phillips in his studies of Hawai'i's Democrats between World War II and 1974. "We are a myth-loving people and it has been a romantic story. Myth, repeated often enough, becomes, in the minds of some, truth." In fact, Phillips wrote, "The 1954 election was the culmination of changing patterns of social and political development with roots in the New Deal legislation which pre-dated World War II." The established powers in the community at that time—the factoring companies, the big trusts, the Republican Party—were insensitive to changes taking place around them, such as the rapid growth of Hawai'i's Asian-ancestry population. "The New Deal was slow in coming to Hawaii, but it was inevitable that it should arrive." That "Deal" is still strongly believed to have benefited those who needed it most at the time, namely, nonwhites.

Hawai'i's Democrats still have a powerful and effective myth-making machine. Although the Republicans have fielded several strong candidates since 1962—the year Hawai'i elected its first Democratic Governor, John A. Burns—the races for governor have rarely been close. Indeed, the only real competition in gubernatorial elections has been between establishment Democrats and the maverick Democrats who have challenged them—and lost. In many regards, this is the real two-party system in post-1954 Hawai'i. The trend of late has been for more Democrats and fewer Republicans to enter local politics. Party membership of the state Legislature from 1983 to 1993 was on average over 90 percent Democrat.

Historical fear of Republican rule is not the only factor keeping political conservatives from gaining local office. Hawai'i Democrats have dominated local politics because they are seen as the party of the people, as a champion of minorities and as associated with the economic prosperity of the mid-1960s and early 1970s. Because winning has led to more winning, Democrats have usually projected a unified image, and they have successfully recruited younger voters. However, increased factionalism—led from time to time by Frank Fasi, Tom Gill, Patsy Mink, Jack Lewin and others—has led some to conclude that the Democratic Party may be losing its edge. "Perhaps the time would not be too far away to see the dominant Democratic Party in Hawai'i as an already spent dormant volcano in the political process," James Wang predicted in 1982.

Republicans, meanwhile, need to shake their image as citizens with moneyed interests, not appear too conservative for Hawai'i, attract new members, deal with their own problems of factionalism and abandon a strategy of targeting only selected districts and allocating resources where it is felt Republicans would be successful. "Unless there is some alteration in its image, the Republican Party will most likely continue to have a narrow base of support," wrote Wang. Their image as financially selfish conservatives connected with the plantation past hurts island Republicans the most. It is also an image that is enforced by fact as well as perception. As UH scholar Michael Haas reports, those from the more affluent groups in Hawai'i do indeed tend to vote Republican and along ethnic lines.

Both parties, James Wang argues, need extensive reform and revitalization. Third parties, meanwhile, have to contend with a formidable challenge of overcoming voters' habits of staying with a two-party system. "These third parties, however, do have impact on the political system," Wang explains. "They serve as watchdogs, pointing out problems and injustices as they see them in the government and society." By the end of the twentieth century, the Green Party and Libertarian Party each frequently ran candidates for most of the state's top elective offices, suggesting that a multiparty system may develop. But, few third-party candidates have been elected as of this writing.

As on the mainland, those who belong to the higher socioeconomic classes and who have better educations vote more often. Politicians themselves are mostly from this group and often hail from a business or legal background. Such people usually have more leisure time to get involved in politics, and they perceive the relationship between involvement and their own interests. According to researchers, the number of citizens participating actively in politics in Hawai'i is actually quite small, ranging from 5 to 17 percent of the state population, a figure which includes people related to politicians and those working on their campaigns out of familial obligation. As on the mainland, voter turnout is dropping. In 1996, a record low 67.9 percent of the registered voting population voted, 10 percent less than in 1994 and 13 percent less than 1992. Voting has declined even as registration is made easier for residents, who can register when they renew their driver's licenses or tear out and mail in widely available, easy-to-use forms in local phone books. Still, Hawai'i's rate of voter turnout and overall involvement in politics is somewhat higher than in most other states.

Until the early 1990s, Democrats could claim pride in their rule, for Hawai'i's economy had largely been one of continuous growth. The rewards, though not shared by all island residents, have been rich. Whites, Japanese, Chinese and Korean Americans in particular have seen their standard of living increase markedly. But in the last decade of the twentieth century, one issue has dominated Hawai'i politics—a troubled state economy, marked by high unemployment, business layoffs and closures, personal and professional bankruptcies, declining tourist numbers and an overwhelming sense that things can never return to the way they were before. Hawai'i's leaders—especially Democrats—have increasingly become the primary target for voter anxiety. There appears to be a growing assumption that socioeconomic prosperity is closely linked to political control. Indeed, both the Republican rule of the first half of the century and the Democratic rule of the latter half were linked to the notion that "to the victor goes the spoils." The overthrow of Republicans in favor of Democrats in the 1950s, while not a revolution, did indeed change the distribution of island largesse. Though the Big Five, Republicans and many powerful institutions that supported the Republican rule continued to do well financially, the Democrats now shared in the economic pie. It is an ironic turnaround for a political party that has long viewed itself as a "party of the people."

If Hawai'i's Democrats can continue to count on votes from those at the bottom of the socioeconomic ladder, the state's recent economic troubles might be viewed as good news for the party. The ranks of the unemployed, those in the lowest-paid service sector jobs of the tourism industry and the ranks of the homeless continue to grow, while the state's greatest wealth is concentrated in the hands of just 22,000 individuals with assets of $600,000 or more. Educational attainments that might lift Hawai'i's poorest residents out of poverty continue to elude many. The state struggles to attract—or create a work force for—forward-looking industries that could generate new revenue streams. Cumbersome and bureaucratic institutions stifle entrepreneurial spirit. Small businesses are closing; large businesses are cutting back or decamping for the mainland. The state's employment base, as well as its revenue streams, is shrinking, virtually ensuring that the "have-not" portion of the population will continue to grow.

The Centers of Power

If Hawai'i is to improve its economy—and the socioeconomic status of its neediest people—a logical place to begin is in the arena of local politics. Money in Hawai'i politics continues to be a profound influence and powerfully limits the ability of the state to address the needs of all its people. That is because local political leadership has been as exclusive as its wealth distribution. The rich continue to get richer, while the rest of the population finds life more financially difficult than ever.

As imperial as Republican rule may have been for the first half of this century, at least it was relatively easy to understand who ran things: the Big Five. Today, the lines of power are more complex. Local political observer Chuck Freedman holds that the "Big Five" of today are the state's two largest banks, Bank of Hawaii and First Hawaiian Bank; the Bishop Estate (an institution with "lofty, charitable ends and a developer's means," says Freedman); the labor unions, with the HGEA and UPW replacing the ILWU as the most influential; the news media (DBEDT estimates that the combined circulation of Honolulu's two dailies totals just under one-fifth of the island population, but editors say that readership is much higher because papers are often read by whole families); and what Freedman calls "the anti-establishment establishment," by which he means community organizations that focus on particular issues. Freedman excludes the visitor industry and foreign investors, neither having emerged as key political players.

Hawaii Business magazine, in an early 1990s report on who has replaced the Big Five, also named the state's two leading banks and Bishop Estate, and included former Big Five member Alexander & Baldwin, which remains a shipping, real estate and agricultural conglomerate; the estate of James Campbell, due to its large land base; Hawaiian Electric Industries, which owns and operates other interests in addition to providing electricity to 95 percent of island residents; Hawaii Medical Service Association (HMSA), the state's largest provider of health-care coverage; and state government. Alexander & Baldwin's total revenues still place it among the state's top five businesses, but the remaining former Big Five organizations are no longer in that company: Theo H. Davies and Co. Ltd. was acquired by Hong Kong's Jardine Matheson and Co. in 1973 and ranks among the top 30 Hawai'i corporations; C. Brewer and Co. Ltd. ranked 27th (in 1997, C. Brewer relocated from Honolulu to Hilo, in hopes of capitalizing on the growth of the Big Island's diversified agricultural crops); the original Castle & Cooke Ltd. is now Dole Food Co. Inc., and is owned by a California real estate developer (while it ranks first among Hawai'i-chartered corporations, only 5 percent of its revenues are generated in Hawai'i and most of its employees live out of the state); and Amfac Inc. was acquired by JMB Realty Corp., a giant Chicago-based real estate corporation.

Political writer Robert M. Rees and *Honolulu Weekly* editor Julia Steele defined power in Hawai'i as the ability to influence events. Its exercise depends on access to decision making. Power in Hawai'i has two dimensions: *mass*, determined by combined factors of money, votes, contacts and the ability to grant favors; and *distance* from the center of decision making—the closer one is to this center, the greater one's power. Rees and Steele, writing in October 1993, listed then-Governor John Waihee, U.S. Senator Daniel Inouye and Honolulu Democratic Party insiders and business leaders such as Tom Enomoto, Daniel K. Arita, Harold Matsumoto and Yukio Takemoto at the center of power. Hawai'i's business establishment is to be found nearby in Rees's "Power Universe." It includes First Hawaiian Bank Chair Walter Dods, then-Bank of Hawaii Chair Howard Stephenson (since succeeded by Lawrence Johnson) and Executive Vice President Dolly Ching, Castle & Cooke Chair David Murdock, C. Brewer Company Chair "Doc" Buyers, Queen Emma Foundation Chair Bob Oshiro and Aloha Airlines founder Hung Wo Ching, among others. Bishop Estate is near this power center, too, as are the Campbell Estate, Outrigger Hotels magnate Richard Kelley, and others.

Rees and Steele argued that the state Legislature and the University of Hawai'i were lacking in real power, while Hawaiian sovereignty groups, including Ka Lāhui and the state Office of Hawaiian Affairs, were large and important but distant from power centers. The islands' major media services, including Honolulu's dailies and television news, are "co-opted" and thus spokespersons for those who actually wield power, though they occasionally are able to affect events. Rees also listed a number of individuals who can of themselves influence events, including Big Island rancher Larry Mehau and various Democratic and Republican politicians.

Though Honolulu's daily newspapers are indeed closely connected to state power centers, in political matters both papers exercise a great deal of influence. It is unusual in this day and age for a morning and afternoon paper still to be competing in the same city, for the national trend has been for evening newspapers to go out of business. But, *The Honolulu Advertiser* and *The Honolulu Star-Bulletin* are unique; until recently, they were even briefly owned by the same corporation. They share the same office building and printer, and they frequently run identical news reports and articles. And, many on the staffs of both papers are in close contact with political and business circles (indeed, the newspapers' offices are only a few blocks from City Hall and the state Capitol). Some feel this symbiotic relationship is not conducive to good journalism. "Under the terms of their joint operating agreement, our dailies have absolutely no incentive to be good newspapers and every incentive not to be," Rees observed. That agreement—a congressionally- approved arrangement exempting the papers from anti-trust laws in order to assist with their survival—is in effect until the year 2012. A.A. Smyser, a senior editor with the *Star-Bulletin*, agrees that there is no incentive for the two newspapers to "go after each other" and that the editorial staffs of both "tend to see things pretty much the same way," though this is not required by the Hawaii Newspaper Association.

The papers' editorial staffs are very much separate. That matter was well illustrated in August 1997, when five island citizens—Senior U.S. District Judge Samuel King, Monsignor Charles Kekumano, retired state Appellate Judge Walter Heen, former Kamehameha School for Girls Principal Gladys Brandt (all part-Hawaiians) and UH Mānoa Law Professor Randall Roth—penned a lengthy critique of four of the five Bishop Estate trustees. The authors took on former legislators Richard "Dickie" Wong and Henry Peters, and Gerard Jervis and Lokelani Lindsey; only trustee Oswald Stender was not criticized. The authors of "Broken Trust" first approached the *Advertiser*'s editors with their manuscript but later published with the *Star-Bulletin*, a major media scoop that resulted in multiple, extensive investigations of the trustees' performance.

"You've got to understand what you've got going here," Frank Fasi complained to *Honolulu* magazine in 1994. "You've got the largest media conglomerate in the country, Gannett, controlling both newspapers.... So I'm saying that the newspapers stand for monopoly—land monopoly, insurance monopoly, banking monopoly. We probably have more monopolies in operation in this state than any other state in the history of the United States." Many candidates for office have complained that the local media favor only well-known candidates who can afford to purchase advertising space and time and that their coverage reflects this. "[T]he fact of the matter is that the *Advertiser* inevitably will provide more coverage of the candidates who have the most active and viable campaigns," explained then-*Advertiser* Editor Gerry Keir about his newspaper's coverage of candidates.

The media, as well their perception of a candidate's resources, thus have a great deal to do with calling attention to who is and is not politically viable. "They have little or no money to buy political advertising, and they get scant media attention," observed *Advertiser* reporter Kevin Dayton of minor candidates. "Newspapers and television generally write them off and focus on those who appear to have more money, more support and a reasonable chance of winning."

There is also the matter of ethnic bias. There are many influential whites in the media, and, though both dailies have increasingly diversified their news coverage, both are also seen as "white" papers. Both have a high number of white readers, acknowledges the Star-Bulletin's Smyser, and readers of both dailies are older and have higher incomes than most of the island population. But the Star-Bulletin has a higher percentage of Japanese and Chinese readers. This is due to the Star-Bulletin's support, at the direction of publishers Joe and Betty Farrington, for statehood in the 1950s, Smyser explains. He suggests that recent increases in Advertiser coverage of Asian Americans, especially Japanese-American experiences during World War II, show that the Advertiser is courting Asian-American readers, many of whom remember that it opposed statehood.

Jerry Burris, an editor with the Advertiser, agrees, explaining that it would be foolish to alienate potential readers. He also agrees with Smyser's generalization about the newspapers' audiences, adding that more males than females read the papers, and readers in general have more education than most island residents. Further, he notes that the Advertiser, though much more enlightened than in pre-statehood days, still rankles some readers, as when former Advertiser publisher Thurston Twigg-Smith expressed his views in print that the overthrow of the monarchy was beneficial to Hawai'i and that sovereignty would not be.

The close relationship between the media and government needs to be considered. For example, Republican gubernatorial candidate Pat Saiki's 1994 communications director, Bob Wernet, had formerly worked for Democratic Governor George Ariyoshi. Before that he was a City Hall reporter for Honolulu television and radio. Advertiser political reporter Peter Rosegg quit journalism after the 1994 election to work in government—

as Governor Ben Cayetano's communications director. He later resigned to join a Honolulu public relations firm. While the practice of moving from one field to another is not uncommon, what arguably *is* uncommon is for a sitting governor to serve as a television political analyst. Yet that is exactly the role John Waihee assumed on election night 1994 for KHON Channel 2 News. In addition to providing commentary on statewide races—including the one for his job—Waihee interviewed his successor, Ben Cayetano, his predecessor, George Ariyoshi, lieutenant governor-elect Mazie Hirono and author Tom Coffman—all Democrats. Waihee praised Cayetano for upholding "Democratic values" and "taking the high road" during the campaign, while local Republicans had made a mistake by following "mainland trends." Waihee would later show up at Cayetano's headquarters (the KHON studios were across the street) to join in the Democrats' victory celebration.

The *Weekly*'s Rees has commented on the effectiveness of other "power centers" in the islands. "The election of neighborhood board members is Hawaii's most meaningless exercise in democracy, rivaled only by our election of the Board of Education," Rees wrote in 1997. Only a third of the ballots mailed to homes of registered voters are returned, and some neighborhood board members are consumed with their self-importance rather than the public good. Other gatherings, however, carry a great deal of weight. *Star-Bulletin* political reporter Richard Borreca cites the annual meeting of over 100 of "Hawaii's elite" who have gathered every year since 1963 to address the state's economy. The participants are drawn from Hawaiʻi's top businesses and educational leaders and include First Hawaiian Bank, Outrigger Hotels, Kamehameha Schools/ Bishop Estate, Alexander & Baldwin and Aston Hotels. "This is where you will meet Hawaii's movers and shakers," Borreca quoted a participant. Actually, most people will *never* meet this group; the meetings have been closed to the public.

Machines and Grass Roots

Honolulu Advertiser political editor Jerry Burris, writing about cronyism in Hawai'i government in the 1990s, noted the observations of a state legislator who speaks of a "Mega Club" involving the political parties, powerful unions, big banks, land trusts and major downtown law firms that keep the club running with their considerable resources. It is the "old boy network"—a label commonly applied to Democratic power brokers—by another name. In Hawai'i, Burris explained, cronyism goes beyond politics. "People in Hawaii (like people in other insular places) tend to deal with each other based on past associations, kinship and shared experience," he said. "To an outsider, this looks like cronyism and it's bad. To an insider, it's 'ohana [family] and it's perfectly natural." Natural or not, in recent years the Democratic Party has been damaged by accusations of political fund-raising abuses, illegal use of funds and government procurement irregularities. "Leaders of the Democratic party have become a 'machine' without any apparent redeeming, progressive cause to advance on behalf of the people they were elected to serve," scholar John C. McClaren writes. "They seem to have lost themselves in their hunger to maintain dominance." Like others, McClaren uses the plantation era as a metaphor to describe the present state of Hawai'i's one-party political dominance. The *nisei* [second-generation Japanese Americans] Democrats have actually become the *"luna,"* or plantation managers, that they sought to eliminate in 1954. "Power and dominance, the worst parts of Hawai'i's plantation system, have survived intact and continue to flourish within Hawai'i's government and its two major political parties," McClaren says.

Despite the dominance of the Democrats, political parties in Hawai'i have become increasingly weak in setting the agenda for elections. A candidate will emerge and declare his or her candidacy and party affiliation far more often than a party will select a certain candidate. Candidates also may abandon party platforms. Nor do people vote strictly on party lines, as they once did. Individual voters and organized interest groups have more say in politics than parties. The primary function of parties today is to organize and recruit candidates for office, according to UH-Hilo scholar James C.F. Wang. "The fact that architects, engineers, developers, contractors and labor unions have become a major source of campaign contributions raises the question of whether these individuals and interest groups have an advantage over the general public in influencing government decisions," Wang writes.

If political parties lack power, it may be because they have lost the ability to decide which candidates and campaigns will be funded. Although power is in the hands of the few, local politicians eagerly embrace the mass populace—if only during election campaigns. The small-town atmosphere of much of Hawai'i lends itself well to such efforts. Rallies that offer food and music in a relaxed atmosphere, or more intimate coffee hours, are common. Roadside sign-waving is said to have started with Charles Campbell, a former city Councilman and state legislator, whose high school students waved signs on the roadside on his behalf in the 1960s. Many are critical of sign-waving, not only because it impedes traffic, but because it does not inform voters in substantive ways. It is unlikely, though, that this widely-used form of campaigning will disappear anytime soon from Hawai'i streets, because it reaches a large number of people quickly and inexpensively. A candidate with union support can count on a large number of sign-wavers. They create the impression that a candidate has a large and enthusiastic following—a strategy that works when candidates are judged by passersby on their popularity rather than political platforms.

James Wang observes that there are at least five types of interest groups that participate in the political process of Hawai'i, each with varying degrees of intensity. They are labor organizations, business associations, professional groups, ethnic and minority associations and public interest groups. Of these, ethnic and minority groups operate subtly, backing candidates only within their groups. Public interest groups lobby for or against a candidate on the basis of a single issue—much like professional associations with considerable financial resources. Unions, meanwhile, remain powerful political forces if an election is close, if unions present a united front or if they have singled out an enemy. However, as noted earlier, rank and file union voting is not necessarily the norm; increasingly, union members choose to vote their conscience.

Local political observer Hubert S. Kimura says that the candidates who spend the most in a campaign are usually the successful ones, but money is not entirely necessary for success if a strong "grass-roots" strategy is chosen. The essence of a grass-roots campaign is the person-to-person delivery of information about a candidate on a block, street or precinct level. It is a particularly successful approach in Hawai'i because of the state's small geographical size. "Irrespective of which office your candidate is seeking, personal contact with the voters is crucial and necessary," Kimura argues in *The Akamai Strategist* (*akamai* means smart or clever). "Personal contact cannot be replaced by computers or television." But money still underpins all campaigns; as Kimura notes, it is often a useful strategy to challenge the source of an opponent's campaign contributions or portray him or her as a rich man's candidate—an appealing strategy to the majority who have little wealth.

Scholar James A. Geschwender observed that grass-roots political initiatives, mostly on O'ahu, have emerged in the past few decades, focused upon issues ranging from environmental protection (Save Our Surf in the mid-1960s and Life of the Land in the 1970s) to public use of state land (Sand Island and Mokauea) and eviction struggles (Oto Camp and Kalama Valley). The Waiāhole-Waikāne water issue of the 1970s, a conflict over O'ahu Windward and Leeward water rights, continues to this day. Geschwender believes these examples indicate that power bases can be created, that power is not a fixed commodity in Hawai'i, that unity is critical to the success of such groups and that such groups must be patient against usually well-funded opposition.

It is not a simple task. As Deborah Chang observes in her study of a group of residents in the Kohala section of the island of Hawai'i, the ethnic and class divisions that were formed during the plantation era do not disappear overnight—or even in several generations. The Kohalans have struggled with large companies, major private landowners and prominent citizens who have the monetary power, administrative skills and personal contacts to influence decisions more easily than the average citizen. "The effects of the old system can be seen in feelings of inferiority and the lack of self-confidence which discourage Kohalans from assuming positions of leadership or unifying to strengthen their political influence," Chang writes. "Political action is then left to those who are thought to be more qualified through experience and education."

Still, Hawai'i does have a history of social activism. Robert H. Mast and Anna B. Mast note in *Autobiography of Protest in Hawai'i* that thousands of state citizens have been and are active in a number of controversial issues, ranging from marijuana cultivation to beach-access rights, from same-sex marriage to abortion, from Hawaiian sovereignty to nuclear power—in spite of the generally-observed rule among local cultures that one should "not make waves" or challenge the status quo. For the most part, though, the centers of power in Hawai'i are entrenched. It is an axiom of local politics that politicians elected to office in Hawai'i may remain there as long as they see fit. Hawai'i's governor and lieutenant governor are limited to two four-year terms each, the only political offices in the state with such limits. "Only ambition for higher office, retirement or death has ever removed a Hawaii legislator," reporter Peter Rosegg observed in 1993. "No member of Congress from Hawaii has ever been voted out of office by the people."

Class Politics

To see how matters of money influence Hawai'i elections in the 1990s, consider the career of Ben Cayetano, a Filipino-American lawyer, former state legislator and descendant of immigrants to the islands. In his first race for governor, Cayetano presented a well-crafted, class-conscious image to the electorate as a kid from the streets in a 30-minute campaign film called "Reach for the Moon." The title came from a warning delivered to a young Cayetano by his mother just before he moved to the mainland in 1963: "Boy, don't reach for the moon." The film was produced by Jack Siegle, who had also produced similar, successful campaign films for former governors Jack Burns, George Ariyoshi and John Waihee, as well as U.S. Senator Dan Inouye.

"Reach for the Moon" featured, among others, attorney Earl Anzai—later Governor Cayetano's budget director—who explained how impressed he was that Cayetano took his elderly father into his home to care for him "in the Japanese tradition." An elderly resident stated in "Reach for the Moon" that before the 1950s, local people had no power. Plantation laborers, though they came voluntarily to Hawai'i, are portrayed as prisoners of the plantations, and Democrats as their liberators. Cayetano's candidacy was thus linked with the Democrats' well-known, if self-told, history. "Republicans always chose money over people's needs," Cayetano himself stated in the film, emphasizing a common Democratic theme. "He's about helping the underdog," said Skippa Diaz, Farrington High School's popular football coach.

Political columnist Dan Boylan called "Reach for the Moon" producer Jack Siegle's best effort. "It's got everything," he noted in *MidWeek*. "Great plot, Cayetano's rise from the mean streets of Kalihi to the lieutenant governorship, some affecting stars in Cayetano's three handsome and well-spoken children.... It also has a basic integrity." Later in the campaign, Boylan grew critical because Cayetano's ads did not reflect his true and admirably combative nature. "His sales people have completely sanitized him," Boylan wrote. "Cayetano's television ads are so slick they almost slide off the screen." *Advertiser* reporter Peter Rosegg observed that the commercial was intended to counter Cayetano's reputation as a "gruff, unsmiling and often angry-seeming politician." It was influenced by advice from mainland consultant Joseph Napolitan, a national political operator with long involvement in Hawai'i Democratic campaigns who has a reputation for "emotionally charged" TV campaigning. "Joe Napolitan was our ace-in-the-hole," admitted Charles Toguchi, Cayetano's campaign manager. "He's never lost a race for governor here."

Remarkably, John Waihee—the governor with whom Ben Cayetano served as lieutenant governor for eight years—did not appear in Cayetano's 30-minute commercial, nor did he appear in Cayetano's campaign literature. Dan Boylan claimed that Cayetano wanted to separate himself from the Waihee administration. "I don't have a campaign to 'distance' myself from John Waihee," Cayetano said well before declaring his candidacy for governor. "I just think that sometimes he's been ill-served by a few people around him who have been giving him bad advice." A high-profile example of Cayetano's disagreements with Waihee was his opposition to Waihee's nomination of Sharon Himeno for a state Supreme Court justice—a nomination the state Senate later rejected. Cayetano also called on former state Budget Director Yukio Takemoto to resign (Takemoto did later resign) due to ethical violations, and argued that Jack Gonzales, executive director of the state Campaign Spending Commission, should step down after Gonzales was indicted (and later convicted) by the federal government in connection with a $10 million fraud scheme.

Cayetano's ads also claimed that the "old boys"—who are never clearly identified but presumably are former and present politicians and businessmen—were abandoning their traditional support for Democrats because they feared the prospect of a governor with whom they had no influence. If he won the election, Cayetano said, "They know the game is over for them." That was an interesting statement from Cayetano, who was well connected to many island leaders, most of whom he had worked closely with in his years in the state Legislature. He had been actively involved with Democratic politics for over 20 years. Cayetano was also greatly helped in 1994 by running mate Mazie Hirono, who had been actively involved with many of the same political circles as Cayetano.

Cayetano's 1994 election demonstrated that union support is critical to Hawai'i elections, especially when they are close, for the candidate with union support benefits from union money and manpower. *Star-Bulletin* reporter Richard Borreca observed that Hawai'i's labor unions are responsible for coining the term "MUDPAC," a political action committee that comes together in the last weeks of a campaign to smear a candidate. "Likely as not it is a campaign waged to help a Democrat, but no Democrat has publicly called for the unions to stop it," he wrote.

Cayetano's 1994 general election opponents complained bitterly about several early union endorsements. Jack Lewin, Cayetano's opponent in the Democratic primary that year, had complained about early union endorsements of Cayetano from the UHPA and the ILWU. Republican Pat Saiki, who lost a close senate race to Democrat Dan Akaka in 1990, also experienced the difficulty of running without union endorsements. Akaka had all of the union endorsements in that Senate race while Saiki had none. Many believed that the efforts of the unions in that campaign's final days contributed to Saiki's loss. As Sam Kuwata, a mainland consultant, explained about the Saiki-Akaka race, a massive outreach effort was launched by the unions. It included phone calls, friend-to-friend letters, brochures and door-to-door canvassing of targeted areas. Hundreds of thousands of letters were mailed during the last weeks of the campaign. "It was an awesome effort," Kuwata said.

The top three gubernatorial candidates in 1994 all aggressively sought union endorsement, but only one candidate received that endorsement— Ben Cayetano. Indeed, Cayetano's labor support was nearly unanimous, as was running mate Mazie Hirono's. Pat Saiki tried in vain to appeal to labor. When that failed, Saiki criticized union endorsements as being merely an extension of Democrats' power. Saiki's pleas to the public, however, fell flat. Moreover, they emboldened union leaders' opposition to her candidacy. UPW state director Gary Rodrigues said Saiki's efforts to portray herself as a friend of the working people were similar to "someone saying he's your friend until it's time to throw you a life raft, but he keeps it himself." HGEA's Executive Director Russell Okata warned that union members should be concerned if Saiki were elected because she was probably considering abolishing jobs, a charge that Saiki denied. Democratic Party State Chair Richard Port suggested that, if elected, Saiki would "systematically attempt to dismantle Hawaii's public and private worker unions." "No, Mrs. Saiki. You're NOT our Friend," proclaimed a newspaper ad paid for by an alliance of unions that called itself Workers for Good Government. The same organization ran a full-page ad the day before the election "apologizing" for not supporting Saiki and independent candidate Frank Fasi and endorsing Cayetano and his running mate. The ad was signed by thousands of union members and a disclaimer stated that the ad was printed without the approval or authorization of any candidate.

Unions did not do all of Cayetano's fighting. He himself stated that Saiki could not "bring labor to the table unless she calls out the National Guard because she's been attacking labor all the time." Cayetano told a group of ILWU delegates that when Saiki was a member of Congress, she had voted against a measure that would have raised the minimum wage to $4.55 an hour. Saiki eventually voted to raise the minimum wage to $4.25. Mary George, a former state legislator and co-chair of Saiki's campaign, said Cayetano's attack was not fair. "If you are the governor, you can bring people to the table," she said. "They have to come. [Cayetano's charge] was a meaningless statement that just reiterated the underlying message that the Democrats as a party have been helpful to labor and kept labor in a position of power."

Cayetano's message succeeded. Saiki was especially stung by HSTA's endorsement of Cayetano. As a former teacher, a graduate of Hilo High School, the mother of five public-school graduates and a founding member of HSTA, Saiki felt she had a claim on the union's endorsement. "It is apparent to me that the HSTA leadership endorses 'business as usual' and wants no change from the status quo," said Saiki, adding that she believed that most teachers actually supported her candidacy. HSTA President Sharon C. Mahoe countered that, compared to Cayetano, Saiki did not have "concrete" answers to HSTA concerns and that Saiki, though a former teacher herself, did not seem to understand teachers' issues. "Most important, she has never said that education would be her first priority," Mahoe explained. "We endorse Ben Cayetano because he will put education first." HSTA's Executive Director George Yamamoto stated that the HSTA would be a "major force" in the 1994 election. Indeed, HSTA made its endorsement in March of that year rather than waiting until June as it had traditionally done. Frank Fasi aide Linda Wong complained about the endorsement, stating that HSTA leaders "railroaded" the Cayetano endorsement in opposition to the views of its members; Fasi was shut out of HSTA's candidate screening process because he failed to meet a newspaper advertisement deadline notifying the public of HSTA's activities. Wong claimed HSTA ignored Fasi because its endorsement was already a "done deal."

Reporter Richard Borreca called the early union endorsement a turning point in the 1994 campaign. At that time, Cayetano trailed Saiki badly in public opinion polls. Because Hawai'i's public school teachers are an important part of the state's political grass roots, HSTA was expected to field more than 1,000 teachers to help Cayetano's campaign with sign-waving, letter writing, phoning friends and helping organize for election day. Borreca also noted that Cayetano was helped in earning teacher union support by Charles Toguchi, a popular former state school superintendent and state legislator who resigned to head Cayetano's campaign. *Star-Bulletin* editorial writer Diane Yukihiro Chang noted that, though Cayetano was to be credited for his development of the "A+" after-school program, he had done little else concerning education during his years as lieutenant governor to John Waihee, who had promised to deliver an education "second to none." Chang interpreted the teacher endorsement as "blatantly subjective and self-serving," an obvious effort to maintain a status quo that nearly everyone agreed needed radical improvement.

Unions made news in other ways in 1994. In April, three bargaining units of Hawai'i's largest public employee union, the HGEA, went on strike, the first strike by the white-collar union in its 60-year history. Nearly 20,000 of HGEA's state employees walked off their jobs and held signs of protest for two weeks until the union and the government could agree on a contract for HGEA units 3, 4 and 13. The strike was a testing ground for the major candidates, yet all were rendered politically ineffectual by the strike. As Honolulu mayor, Frank Fasi was in the position of being one of the targets of the strikers. Cayetano was linked to the Waihee administration that led the state and counties in negotiations with the union. Saiki, meanwhile, was saddled with a reputation for not caring about unions. The *Star-Bulletin*'s Borreca observed that the strike was a potentially critical opportunity for the gubernatorial candidates—the strikers were essentially the same kinds of people (that is, mostly women) who so generously volunteer their services for local campaigns—but the top candidates were "low key" in their approach to the strike. Nevertheless, by August, the HGEA would endorse Cayetano. Fasi was deemed too confrontational for the HGEA. Saiki's political philosophy—specifically her support of Presidents Reagan and Bush—was incompatible. State health director Jack Lewin, campaigning for the Democratic nomination for the governor's job, was believed to be too inexperienced. However, HGEA's unity was somewhat suspect. Ed Nishioka, chairman of the Frank Fasi-organized Best Party, argued that the Maui HGEA chapter supported Fasi. A *Star-Bulletin* reporter interviewed several union members from the HGEA and HSTA who were upset that their unions had "spoken" for their members without properly consulting them. Some pointed out that Jackie Young, a longtime HGEA member and onetime union steward, was snubbed in favor of Mazie Hirono in the Democratic lieutenant governor race.

Cayetano's union support was not uniform elsewhere. Columnist Dan Boylan, who teaches at UH-West O'ahu, noted that many in his own union, UHPA, voted for Jack Lewin in the 1994 Democratic primary and split their votes in the general election, though UHPA officially endorsed Ben Cayetano. Still, UHPA leaders John Radcliffe and R. Sinikka Hayasaka dismissed Pat Saiki's charges that UHPA's endorsement, like HSTA's, was merely "old boy network" politics. Explaining UH professors' reluctance to vote for Cayetano, Boylan wrote, "Cayetano comes from a class of people that are not very highly thought of. Filipinos do the lawn work in Nu'uanu and Kāhala [affluent Honolulu neighborhoods]. Many whites are not used to considering Filipinos to be smart. But, even though Cayetano is not a typical Filipino, his middle-class aspirations and his hard work are an American story that many non-whites can relate to. For a lot of local people, this was their story, too." That story involves taking care of constituents. Cayetano's victory was linked to the economic hopes of much of the electorate, which had been in trouble for three years. As a sign on the Wai'anae Coast read, "Vote Dem, Save Job."

Buying the Vote

The 1994 campaigns of Ben Cayetano, Pat Saiki and Frank Fasi constituted the most expensive governor's race in Hawai'i's history, costing a total of nearly $10 million. *State Government News* reported that the candidates spent $25.29 per voter in

1994 —compared to the national average of $6.96 for the 36 states that held gubernatorial elections that year. The report explained that California and Texas are consistently the most expensive places to run for governor—over *five times* more expensive than Hawai'i—but Hawai'i's candidates in 1994 spent more money over a much smaller population. Saiki officially spent the most—$3.6 million, followed by Cayetano ($2.9 million) and Fasi ($2.3 million). Official campaign spending reports can be misleading, however. Cayetano did not report the considerable spending by other Democrats or labor unions on his behalf. Either through monetary contributions or through cooperative advertising, all of the top gubernatorial candidates received help from their respective political parties. Many political observers, including Tom Coffman, argue that Fasi in fact spent the most money during the 1994 campaign. Jack Lewin, Cayetano's main Democratic primary opponent, raised and spent only about a quarter of a million dollars. He refused to accept contributions from special interests and his fundraising was hampered by his late entry into the campaign.

Of the roughly $3 million spent by each top candidate, a remarkable proportion came from the same donors. "Most of the money came in big bundles from vested interests who have a stake in the good will of the political system," according to *The Honolulu Advertiser*. "Indeed, a close look at campaign spending records would indicate that many big contributors gave to all three candidates." Local political writer and historian Bob Dye notes that the *Advertiser* later exposed contributions of "bundled" donations to Cayetano's 1994 campaign. Bundling is the all-too-common practice of making a campaign contribution beyond the legal limit by donating funds, goods or services in the name of another person such as family members or co-workers. The *Advertiser* noted that former campaigns of John Waihee and Frank Fasi had also received bundled donations.

Fasi and Cayetano also had the advantage of incumbency in 1994. It is common for staff members of elected officials to contribute to their bosses' campaigns. A number of city cabinet members appointed by Fasi while he was Honolulu mayor contributed the maximum individual amount allowed by law ($2,000), as did a number of Lieutenant Governor Cayetano's appointees. Some appointees seek more aggressive ways to support their bosses. City wastewater director Kenneth Rappolt, who donated $1,000 to Fasi's gubernatorial campaign, admitted in June of 1994 that he had asked his former private-sector employer for contributions to both Fasi's campaign for governor and Jeremy Harris's campaign for Honolulu mayor in return for a $400,000 contract, which they would reward without competitive bidding. Rappolt resigned and was later convicted of illegal fund-raising activities and mail fraud. The *Advertiser* also noted that much of Fasi's $3 million war chest came from people and companies doing business with the city. For his part, Fasi accused Saiki and Cayetano of "selling out" Hawai'i by raising part of their treasuries on the mainland.

High spending is not unique to the governor's race. Jeremy Harris and Arnold Morgado each had campaign treasuries of over half a million dollars in the 1994 and 1996 Honolulu mayoral races, considerably more than their opponents had. The money they spent appeared to have been a factor in the mayoral outcome: Harris finished first in both races against the second-place Morgado.

Despite the large sums of money spent on behalf of all three 1994 gubernatorial candidates, Ben Cayetano and the Democrats successfully portrayed Pat Saiki and the Republicans as a party of and for the rich, incapable of relating to the average working person. "The Democratic Party is concerned with people, and the Republican Party is concerned with money," Cayetano charged early in the campaign. A few months later, he said, "[Saiki] will not be able to hide from her sorry record of preferential service for her elitist friends at the expense of the common people." It was the "common" people to whom Cayetano appealed to the most. "It's going to be up to you folks here in Kalihi," he told a crowd at Kapalama

Elementary School. Wearing a *palaka* or plaid shirt to symbolize his own working-class roots in the same neighborhoods, Cayetano said his early life was marked by fist fights and pool halls. He left Kalihi at age 18 for Los Angeles, where he earned a bachelor's degree from UCLA and a law degree from Loyola University before returning to Hawai'i.

Cayetano hammered away at his populist ideal. "As a new generation carries us into the next century, we Democrats continue to build on this legacy of social justice, human dignity and individual freedom," the Democratic platform read. Some of this was wishful rhetoric, an effort to put on a unified front while disguising a fractured party. Republicans, sensing the frustration of many voters, charged that Democrats were responsible for putting the state in its worst economic crisis in history, officials under the Waihee-Cayetano administration were politically corrupt, new ideas were needed to diversify and expand the economy, little was being done to include Hawai'i in the rapidly expanding economies of Pacific Rim nations, Republicans were indeed friends of labor, businesses were being strangled by governmental bureaucracy and the size of government in Hawai'i had grown unmanageable. "The main difference between Republican and Democratic philosophy is this: Democrats believe their party and big government can think for you better than you can think for yourself," wrote John D. Ellis, second vice chairman of Hawai'i's Republican Party. "Republicans believe we are all entitled to make our own choices in life without intimidation and with responsibility."

Republicans had on their side several recent embarrassments for Hawai'i's Democrats, including scandals, investigations and missteps. Two state senators both claimed to be state Senate President in 1994, revealing intense factionalism and legislative disarray, and an FBI search was launched over charges that legislators had solicited bribes. A state Senate investigation into the purchasing practices of the state government resulted in the early retirement of the state's budget and finance director. Such wounds prompted Hawai'i's most prominent and powerful Democrat, U.S. Senator Dan Inouye, to endorse Cayetano more than ten months prior to the general election.

Frank Fasi also used a Democratic strategy, focusing on his long-time support for "the little guy." He repeatedly challenged Pat Saiki to reveal her campaign contributors in order to show where Saiki's money came from, presumably to reveal to the public Saiki's "fat cat" connections. The tactic might also frighten away other potential contributors with a threat of public exposure. To reinforce his populist appeal, Fasi used in his campaign materials the "shaka" symbol, a local hand gesture that indicates a salutation or affirmation. The shaka resonates with a large segment of people to whom Fasi was appealing—the "local," underprivileged voter. The shaka, colored in bold yellow and black, had been used in many of Fasi's past campaigns. "You won't see it in boardrooms, but you'll see it on the docks," observes Carole Goodson, a Honolulu graphic designer. In the end, Fasi and Saiki only took votes away from each other and ensured Cayetano's election.

Cayetano's election was clearly a "class" victory. Nearly one out of every two Kalihi voters voted for Democrat Ben Cayetano, with one in three voting for Best Frank Fasi. Cayetano and Fasi thus both attracted more low-income voters than Saiki. About 40 percent of voters in the economically depressed Hilo area favored Cayetano as well, with Fasi and Saiki each getting less than 30 percent. Almost half of all Wai'anae voters chose Fasi, with Cayetano receiving about 30 percent and Saiki about 15 percent. Fasi thus had strong support among Hawaiians and low-income whites. Fasi and Saiki split the Kona-Kohala area at just over 30 percent each with Cayetano somewhat behind, suggesting that middle-class white votes were split three ways, but that Cayetano was least favored. Saiki took the Kāhala-Wai'alae area with over a third of the total vote, thus doing well with affluent whites and

Asians. The more educated the voter, the more likely he or she was to vote for Saiki; the less educated were more likely to vote for Cayetano or Fasi. The area with the most troubled economy due to the closure of agriculture—Hilo—voted for the incumbent party, while the area with the highest unemployment—Wai'anae—voted for a non-traditional third party.

Cayetano was elected governor with just over one-third of the vote (134,978 votes), Saiki and Fasi each receiving somewhat less than one third (107,908 and 113,158 votes, respectively). The Democrats' support was quite small, considering that only 50 percent of eligible citizens actually registered to vote, 77 percent of registered voters did vote and only 36 percent of the vote went to Cayetano and his running mate, Mazie Hirono. But it was enough to win. One observer even argued that, in spite of these low numbers, Cayetano's victory was inevitable. Richard Borreca noted after the primary election that Cayetano had received 40 percent of the island vote. At least one-third of the 30 percent that Jack Lewin earned in the primary would likely go to Cayetano in the general election, leaving him—theoretically—with 50 percent of the vote and Fasi and Saiki splitting the other 50. The election did not turn out precisely as Borreca predicted, but the primary proved to be a strong indicator of who would get the most votes in the general election.

The Party Challenge

On the one hand, Ben Cayetano's victory in 1994 can be seen as an endorsement of Hawai'i's Democratic party. His campaign director Charles Toguchi said that exit polls showed Cayetano was the second choice of those who voted for Pat Saiki or Frank Fasi, indicating that Cayetano would have won even if it had been a two-party race. On the other hand, almost *two-thirds* of the votes went against Cayetano, a fact that can be interpreted to mean that a majority of Hawai'i voters wanted a change from Democratic rule, as many public opinion polls had suggested (but then, these are the same voters who 90 percent of the time reelect incumbents).

Cayetano's victory is also remarkable because he was far behind in public opinion polls until only the last few months of the campaign. This "underdog" status, combined with his tireless, patient campaign style, may have helped Cayetano win. The Democrats were able to do in the last weeks of the campaign what they have often done in the past 40 years—present themselves as the party of the people of Hawai'i. "We were among the people who fought for a new, more equitable way of life—and won," read an ad featuring members of the "Dream Team" of 1954—retired judge Walter Heen, former lieutenant governor and judge Nelson Doi, retired chief justice Bill Richardson, retired justice Ed Nakamura, and former lieutenant governor Tom Gill. The inheritors of that dream—Cayetano, Hirono, U.S. Senator Dan Akaka, and U.S. Representatives Neil Abercrombie and Patsy Mink—were pictured in a similar ad.

Though still in power, the Democrats are in a state of flux. "The 1994 Democrats are a variegated group," observed Dan Boylan after attending the party's convention. "They're whiter, browner, less Japanese-American than I've seen them in the 22 years I've been attending their conclaves.... The generation of Nisei warriors who provided the Party its backbone during most of the last 40 years was little in evidence." Instead, Boylan noted, the party is heavily white-collar, mostly political appointees, state workers, lobbyists and a few extremists. From a party described by ethnic labels, the Democrats had become one whose prominent characteristics are related to socioeconomic class.

The Republicans, meanwhile, continue to ride on the coattails of a single candidate. "Because their chances for net gains in the Legislature are zero, the Republican strategy is to rejuvenate the party not from the grass roots up but from the top down," Robert M. Rees observed during the 1994 campaign. Bob Dye agreed, noting that many major seats went essentially unchallenged. "The past Republican strategy—to target one major race, rather than to support a full slate—has failed," wrote Dye. "The time has come for Republicans to become a full-service political party again." Hawai'i Republicans' inability to field strong candidates for more than one or two races was well symbolized in the candidacy of Robert Garner, who challenged Patsy Mink for Hawai'i's 2nd district seat in the U.S. House of Representatives. Garner gained national attention when local media declared him "missing"—when he chose not to talk to the press, nor even advertise his candidacy. Local Republican officials claimed that they barely even knew Garner, though he earned 22 percent of the vote to Mink's 64 percent in the general election.

The Republican Party also did what it has done throughout the past 40 years—target only selected representative districts. With only a few exceptions, all the targeted districts are on O'ahu, and nearly all comprise the wealthiest concentrations of Hawai'i residents. As might be expected, Pat Saiki did very well in many of these districts, as Republicans usually do. Saiki would have done well in these districts whether she campaigned there or not. Instead, she might better have spent time, money and energy on districts where she was not expected to do well. Democrats won these districts in 1994, as they have in elections past. Targeting key districts is a reliable strategy for Democrats, as well as Republicans. Charles Toguchi explains that the 1994 Cayetano campaign targeted districts—for example, Kalihi and Waipahu, heavily-Filipino neighborhoods—received a great deal of attention, but not Kailua, a heavily-white community. "You've got to get the biggest bang for the buck," Toguchi says. However, Democratic activist Amefil Agbayani says that candidates should not waste their time and money in districts where they have not previously spent time courting voters. "If I had been advising Pat Saiki, I would have told her to stay away from Kāhala and Kalihi," she says. Instead, Agbayani says candidates should concentrate on "swing voters," that is, people who still might be persuaded to vote for a particular candidate.

"One of the reasons Ben won is that there's still enough Republican mythology left in this community and people still respond to it," said Saiki's media advisor, Keith Rollman, the morning after the election. "It's like the Big Five still exist, the cane fields still exist." This rationale was in the minds of not a few Saiki supporters following the election. Democrats, too, saw the election as yet another affirmation of the 1954 revolution and the party of Hawai'i's diverse people. "There's no machine, no body of elders, but people believe this—especially conservative and liberal whites—because it makes them feel better," explained Dan Boylan. "They just can't accept the fact that honest, decent, brown, white, whatever people voted rationally for the Democrats. Cayetano's victory represents democracy." Boylan added that another reason Cayetano won was that the state economy was not nearly as poor as public opinion polls and newspaper reports suggested it was. "Things are not as bad as people say they are, so there was no reason to 'throw the bums out,'" he said, although within only a few months of the 1994 election most observers—including Boylan—acknowledged the seriousness of Hawai'i's moribund economy.

Problems with the Republican Party are also cited. "The Republicans lack a plan," observed Robert M. Rees. "The party likes to refer to itself as a 'Big Tent' that can accommodate different ideas, but this is only a euphemistic metaphor and rationale for continuing to embrace as Republicans the Social Darwinists and Christian Coalition of the 1990s." As if to prove Rees right, after the election Jared Jossem suggested changing the name of the party he chaired to make it easier for people to accept voting for its candidates. "A lot of people tell me they believe in the Republican Party platform, but hesitate to join because they don't want to insult parents and grandparents who have always been Democrats." Political writer Tom Coffman noted that a critical factor in Pat Saiki's defeat was Jossem himself. In his role as an attorney for the Hawaii

Employers Council, which negotiates contracts between unions and businesses, Jossem angered union leaders. This, according to Coffman, "managed to reprise all the historic problems of the Republican Party." Coffman believes Saiki was an ideal candidate to break the Republican's image problem with unions because of her local roots, but Jossem reinforced that negative image. "That's why all the union guys got off their butts, and they made the difference in the election," he said.

"It's to the advantage of Democrats to keep this hatred of Republicans going, to 'emotionalize' the plantation period, because it keeps them in power," Pat Saiki said. "Voters can't seem to let go of the dogma of the Democrats being the party of the 'little people.'" Like the plantations before them, Democrats and unions in particular use their "underground network to spread fear and intimidation" among voters who might consider choosing Republicans or third-party candidates. At least one Democrat acknowledges the staying power of the plantations. "Politics in Hawai'i has never escaped a view based on the plantation image...this view that a handful of people, namely whites, control things, and that the Republican Party wants to bring this back," says former state legislator David Hagino.

That view still has a powerful hold on Hawai'i voters' imaginations. Occasionally, Republican candidates paint themselves as "little people" to win in Democratic stronghold districts. That strategy might not have worked for ex-schoolteacher Pat Saiki, even if she had tried it in 1994, in her quest for statewide office, but it appears to have some power in localized races. Ultimately, it may prove to be a better strategy for a Republican Party ready to abandon a top-down approach and build a grass-roots movement. In the end, some said, Saiki's campaign resembled the rampage of a circus elephant named "Tyke" that escaped from Honolulu's Blaisdell Center in late August of 1994 after killing her trainer. The elephant, of course, is the traditional symbol of the Grand Old Party. Tyke was brought down in the nearby industrial neighborhood of Kaka'ako by 86 rounds from police.

COLOR: "LOOK FOR THE SKIN"

GOVERNOR JACK BURNS once said that Hawai'i's multicultural harmony could be maintained only so long, as no single racial group ever comprised 51 percent of the population. Burns's assertion may never be tested, but evidence shows that—although Hawai'i comprises many races and no single race constitutes a majority—the state has never chosen a member of a numerically small ethnic group for governor. UH history professor Richard Rapson believes Burns's warning was actually a fallacy and an indication of the fragility of race relations in Hawai'i. "It suggested that racial tolerance was not based so much upon affection and trust as upon the sheer demographic inability of any ethnic group to do what it would quickly do if the numbers added up differently: exploit the others."

In Hawai'i, race does matter—especially in politics—but there is little agreement upon *why* and *how much* it matters. However, it is clear from past elections that politicians garner considerable votes based on their race or ethnicity alone. Indeed, "racial balance" is often the first consideration of individuals and parties assembling slates of candidates. Race alone will not get a candidate elected to office, but a politician must court the various racial constituencies that exist in Hawai'i, even those with whom he or she is identified. It also helps to have been born and brought up in the islands; voters are far more inclined to vote for a "local" than a "mainlander."

The term "race" has come to mean something distinctly different in Hawai'i than in most places, including the mainland United States. Race is constructed in Hawai'i *socially* and *culturally*, not biologically. It can appear and be widely recognized or, in some cases, shift and even disappear within a single generation. Sociologist Andrew W. Lind believes that the Hawai'i experience confirms what has been forgotten elsewhere—that the significance of skin color is a human invention. Still, skin color (as well as eye and hair color) means significant things to many people in the islands. "Hawaii cannot be understood without coming to terms with race," writes Richard L. Rapson in *Fairly Lucky You Live Hawaii!* "It is the cornerstone of practically everything that occurs here."

Race or ethnic relations cannot be described in simple terms, though many have done so, usually stating that relations between groups in Hawai'i are as mild as the weather. Hawai'i's plantation system is critical to understanding race relations, just as it is in understanding socioeconomic class relations. It is not so much income or occupation or education which determines one's friends, voting affiliation or prospects for power and prestige, Lawrence H. Fuchs explains in *Hawaii Pono*. "In the forty years following annexation, the peoples of Hawaii thought of themselves, not primarily as doctors, lawyers, druggists, or field hands—or even as Americans— but as haoles, Hawaiians, Portuguese, Chinese, Japanese, and Filipinos." There is considerably more racial and ethnic intermingling today in the islands than at the time Fuchs wrote, and self-identification varies widely among residents. Yet, old ethnic patterns remain strong. While the rest of the United States lumps people of Asian or Pacific heritage together in one "Asian/Pacific" ethnic category, and people of European ancestry together as "white" or "Caucasian," Hawai'i generally retains the classifications that date back to plantation days: Hawaiian, Haole, Chinese, Japanese, Okinawan, Korean, Filipino, Portuguese. Newer arrivals—Samoan, Tongan, Maori, Thai, Vietnamese—are generally not subsumed into the plantation-era designations, but retain the national or cultural ("ethnic") identity they or their forebears brought to the islands. Whether it is a blessing or a curse, this particularized way of looking at race/ethnicity is pervasive in Hawai'i.

Compared with many other places, race relations in Hawai'i *are* relatively benign. While tensions do exist, the islands are not marked by the intense racial turmoil common in other multicultural communities. Race relations in Hawai'i thus invite the question, "How do they all get along?" It is a difficult question to answer, but local politics is an appropriate place to search. Michael Haas, UH professor of political science, wrote in his examination of institutional racism in Hawai'i that political strategies of accommodation, neutralization and polarization used by those in power and out have helped ease tensions and could be used to shed light on improving ethnic relations throughout the world. Haas believes that ethnic inequality is the "well-spring" of important social problems, and that in Hawai'i there is at least a consensus to increase equality across ethnic groups. "The mainland and the world are very much like Hawaii," he says in *Institutional Racism: The Case of Hawaii*. "We live on a small planet, where misbehavior in one place adversely affects the quality of life elsewhere, and where the pursuit of social justice for the least privileged brings benefits to all."

Race Politics

As noted in the preceding chapter, issues of race and socioeconomic class are intertwined. Ethnic heritage is not an automatic or unchangeable marker of class in Hawai'i, but the most privileged group is made up largely of whites, Japanese Americans and descendants of the Hawaiian *ali'i*. Further, there appears to be little chance for those at the bottom of the class hierarchy ever to climb to the top, or even to the comforts of middle-class status. The hierarchy of color applies to Hawai'i politics as well. While election of candidates hailing from diverse backgrounds is another step on the long road toward racial equality, Hawai'i (like the rest of the United States) has a long way to go before roughly equal representation is a reality. Additionally, Hawaiian nationalism complicates island politics and could critically affect the delicate balancing act that characterizes local politics, even while the aim of sovereignty is to elevate the status of the island's most oppressed, impoverished people.

Michael Haas and Peter P. Resurrection in *Politics and Prejudice in Contemporary Hawaii* point to two issues in the early 1970s that illustrate a rising race consciousness. The first occurred in 1971, when Matsuo Takabuki, a Japanese American, was appointed to serve as a trustee of the Bishop Estate. The estate of Princess Bernice Pauahi Bishop was left to support the education system established under her will— the famed Kamehameha Schools—for Hawai'i's children. Hawaiian organizations complained a non-Hawaiian should not be on a board that oversees a private trust for Hawaiians. The second incident occurred during the summer of 1974, when the University of Hawai'i Board of Regents decided to name a new social sciences building after a deceased UH psychology professor, Stanley D. Porteus. A number of people and organizations opposed this, as they interpreted some of Porteus' writings on Hawai'i's people as racist and sexist. Despite the uproar, however, the building was named after Porteus. After renewed protests in the late 1990s, the UH Regents moved in 1998 to change the building's name.

Such incidents as these call renewed attention to the race and class consciousness that originated in the island plantation system. "It was inevitable that ethnic politics should be important in Hawaii, just as it is in large multi-ethnic cities on the mainland," says Lawrence W. Fuchs. "In Hawaii, where the tradition of racial aloha and actual widespread intermarriage often prevented overt expressions of racial prejudice, ethnic tensions frequently found their way into the voting booth." Fuchs points to studies that showed how all major ethnic groups tend to favor their own kind in voting, a practice known as "plunking." "American politics, based upon universal suffrage and competition between political factions, was one of the major by-products of haole civilization, yet participation in Island politics paradoxically linked the natives to the past," Fuchs explains about early twentieth-century Hawai'i. "In an atmosphere sometimes heavy with Puritanism, politics provided welcome respite for Hawaiians. No political speech could begin unless preceded by entertainment, and many Hawaiians looked upon political campaigns as opportunities to break into song and hula. The Hawaiians, as the largest voting group in the Islands, loved the pageantry aimed at recalling the past that aspiring politicians consistently presented."

Racial politics began in nineteenth-century Hawai'i. During the monarchy period, David Kalākaua challenged Prince William Charles Lunalilo after the death of King Kamehameha V in 1872. Kalākaua supporters circulated a paper which tried to show that Lunalilo was not of the Kamehameha line and, furthermore, that he had been misled by foreigners. Kalākaua also charged that, if elected, he would repeal all personal taxes and put native Hawaiians into government jobs. The attack on Lunalilo's birthright backfired, however, and Lunalilo was elected king.

Race and politics were connected in other periods of Hawaiian history as well. "Territorial status mandated one elective office, that of the delegate to Congress," according to Dan Boylan, "and the first man to hold it scared the hell out of the haole elite that ruled the Territory. His name was Robert

Wilcox, his weapon was the Home Rule Party, and his politics of self-determination an abhorrence to the minority of whites whose claim to government was at best shaky. In 1895 Wilcox had attempted to overthrow the republic by force. To haole businessmen, he was a dangerous man indeed.... So they turned to Prince Jonah Kuhio Kalanianaole. In 1902 they succeeded in persuading him to run for delegate as a Republican. He beat Wilcox easily."

Racial politics delayed statehood. L.A. Thurston, W.F. Dillingham and other pre-statehood business and political powers often pointed to fears of an Asian-dominated territorial Legislature in their opposition to statehood. Edward Joesting reports that some politicians in Washington, D.C., had similar concerns. Hawai'i was considered "too Oriental" and "not Western in thought," as well as "dominated" by Communists. Some Hawaiians feared that statehood would move them yet another step away from the days of the monarchy; they, too, worried about Asian domination. It is ironic that non-Asians of the era so feared Asian domination, for Asians had great difficulty exercising political power in the first half of this century. It was not until 1920 that a Chinese descendant was elected to office, and 1930 when two men of Japanese ancestry were elected to the territorial Legislature. The inability to get an Asian elected was partly due to the relatively small numbers of Asians in Hawai'i at this time. Their numbers grew, but after the 1930s their political representation remained disproportionately low.

Dan Boylan argues in *Politics and Public Policy in Hawaii* that ethnicity plays a very strong role in contemporary politics and elections in Hawai'i. "How major ethnic groups will vote is the first consideration in a major race," Boylan quotes a Democratic operative as saying. "I don't think we have to be apologetic about that, because wherever you go in America it's the first rule. 'Birds of the same feather flock together.'" Hawai'i remains in denial about racial politics, said Boylan, though island residents all agree that winning elections means constructing coalitions that appeal to a variety of ethnic groups. This denial is related in part to "expediency and good taste," says Boylan. "In a society so ethnically diverse, one in which no ethnic group dominates, politicians have recognized that ethnic considerations must be limited to the back rooms where they gather to forge campaign strategy."

Islands of Diversity

According to the 1990 Census for Hawai'i, 33.4 percent of island residents are white, 22.3 are Japanese, 15.2 are Filipino, and 12.5 are Hawaiian or part-Hawaiian, with the remaining 16.6 percent comprised of Chinese and others. In terms of their respective percentages, the populations of African Americans, Vietnamese, American Indians, Eskimos and Aleuts in Hawai'i have all increased considerably in recent years, but their overall population numbers remain small; the more notable increases are for whites and Filipinos, whose numbers have grown at roughly the same pace. Filipino and Korean numbers are increasing throughout the state, while white numbers are increasing on the islands of Hawai'i, Maui and Kaua'i. Low birth rates of Chinese and Japanese, meanwhile, account for declines in their population percentages.

Population statistics, however, vary considerably depending on the demographic source, particularly numbers for the white and part-Hawaiian populations. According to the state Department of Health (DOH)—the only other government agency that officially tracks demographics—numbers for whites, Japanese and Filipinos are *lower* than Census Bureau statistics; indeed, white numbers are nearly 10 percent less. The numbers of Hawaiians and part-Hawaiians, meanwhile, are higher, totaling 18 percent. Whether a person with Hawaiian blood chooses to identify as a Hawaiian is largely that person's choice. This has led to much confusion about the precise number of part-Hawaiians. Scholars Herbert Barringer and Patricia O'Hagan listed the 1986 Hawaiian population at 17.2 percent. Of this population, which numbers just over 200,000, less than 5 percent are "pure" or 100 percent Hawaiian; as a percentage of the entire state population, pure Hawaiians are less than 0.1 percent, according to sociologist Kiyoshi Ikeda's 1980s study of Hawaiian population numbers.

Demographic surveys at the city and county level vary as well. The reasons for these variations can be explained in part by different approaches to census taking. The U.S. Census Bureau (from which the Department of Business, Economic Development and Tourism, or DBEDT, receives its numbers for Hawai'i) uses procedures that may work well for much of the U.S. mainland—which is three-fourths white—but they do not work as well in diverse communities. The DOH, therefore, uses its own census criteria in an attempt to more accurately count and categorize Hawai'i's people. For example, the white or Caucasian category as reported by the DOH, excludes Portuguese. There is a separate category for people of Portuguese ancestry, except in marriage categories, where they are combined with whites. In all sections, the category "Hawaiian" also includes "Part-Hawaiian." As in the U.S. Census, ethnicity for the DOH survey is self-reported. The result is that DOH surveys are more detailed than Census statistics. It is not clear, however, if they are more reliable.

Census taking has a long history in Hawai'i. Big Island legend has it that around A.D. 1600, a Hawaiian leader ordered his people to each bring a stone to the base of a mountain so that they might be enumerated. A *heiau*, or sacred place of worship, was created from the stones. The first modern census was conducted throughout the islands in the early 1800s, and the Hawaiian government enacted legislation requiring an annual census by the 1840s.

Demographer Eleanor Nordyke explains that the classification of part-Hawaiians has been modified over the years. In the middle of the nineteenth century the U.S. Census applied the terms "native" and "half-native," and from 1860 to 1890 used the term "half-castes." From 1910 to 1930 the Census Bureau attempted to differentiate between "Caucasian-

Hawaiians" and "Asiatic-Hawaiians." From 1940 to 1960, the Census Bureau and the DOH reported any admixture as "Part-Hawaiian," but in 1970 they both eliminated the traditional distinctions of full-Hawaiian and part-Hawaiian, as pure-blooded Hawaiians were by then few in numbers. Part-Hawaiians were thus merged into the single category of "Hawaiian" or classified with other races. Nordyke also believes that Hawaiians and part-Hawaiians may be undercounted by the U.S. Census, and overcounted by the DOH.

The federal Office of Management and Budget in 1997 revised racial and ethnic reporting categories used by the Census Bureau and other agencies to include a new category for Native Hawaiians, multiracial and multiethnic people in future Census reports. Hawai'i's U.S. Senator Dan Akaka had pushed for the change, mainly to prevent Hawaiians from "falling through the cracks" of federal programs and civil rights laws because they are undercounted. Sovereignty groups such as Ka Lāhui and the state's Office of Hawaiian Affairs supported the measure. State statistician Robert C. Schmitt, however, calls Census distinctions "inevitably meaningless" because *two-fifths* of Hawai'i's resident marriages and nearly *three-fifths* of the babies born to civilian couples are interracial. Schmitt estimates that about one-third of all Hawai'i residents today are of mixed ancestry, and the trend is for increased mixture to a point where Schmitt believes racial and ethnic distinctions will be irrelevant.

One thing that can be agreed upon is that Hawai'i is ethnically diverse. GTE Hawaiian Telephone's 1997 O'ahu white pages, for example, list the most common family names as Lee, Wong, Kim, Johnson, Nakamura, Smith, Ching, Young, Chang, Yamamoto, Higa, Souza, Sato and Silva. The number of Kims has tripled since 1965. The Census Bureau reported that as of 1996, over 15 percent of Hawai'i's population was foreign-born, compared with 10 percent for the entire United States. Hawai'i's current Supreme Court is the most diverse in the country. The five-member court is made up of Chief Justice Ronald Moon (of Korean ancestry) and associate justices Robert Klein (part-Hawaiian), Steven Levinson (white), Paula Nakayama (Japanese-American) and Mario Ramil (Filipino-American). In Hawai'i, there are at least six English daily newspapers, four foreign language or bilingual daily newspapers and several weekly and semi-weekly papers for special audiences. Radio and TV stations broadcast primarily in English, but many programs are aired in Japanese, Mandarin and Cantonese, Korean, Hawaiian, Samoan and in the Philippine dialects of Ilocano and Tagalog. There are in Hawai'i 25,489 who speak Chinese at home, 26,283 who speak Ilocano, 69,587 Japanese speakers and 55,341 Tagalog speakers. Nearly all of them speak English well or very well in addition to their native language.

The Local Factor

The tendency for the people of a region to share similar values and beliefs is quite common. In Hawai'i, a "local" identity operates in a way similar to that of other communities but with a multicultural influence that is different. It is obvious in habits such as taking off shoes before entering a household, eating with chopsticks, giving a floral *lei* on special occasions, and so forth. However, there is another side to local identity, a side that unites some while it keeps others out. "For some, a 'local' is someone born and brought up in Hawaii regardless of race or social background," explains Dennis M. Ogawa's *Kodomo no tame ni.* "For others, the term has a racial connotation and is used to distinguish nonwhite or 'local people' from white people." Ogawa believes the local identity attaches to anyone who is sensitive to the racial and cultural forces operating in Hawai'i. "It means that they share a special language, a special mode of behavior, a special value system, and a special racial experience which separates them and other 'locals' from the 'outsiders.'"

"The term may be used to separate island-born members of ethnic groups from new immigrants; it also brings together the Hawaii-born opposition to Haoles," explains writer John

Kirkpatrick. "Insofar as the label is associated with shared experiences, a history of struggle, and easy, egalitarian social relations, it tends not to apply to any Haole, whether immigrant or Hawaii-born."

Wayne S. Wooden in *What Price Paradise?* identifies a number of characteristics of local people versus nonlocal. Among these, the local: identifies with a blend of various ethnic cultures, feels a strong emotional attachment to Hawai'i, speaks Pidgin as well as Standard English, eats many ethnic foods, has a tanned complexion, has black or brown hair, blames influential organizations for Hawai'i's economic problems, believes the role of women is to care for the family and earn additional income, is a member of the working-to-middle class and believes that Hawai'i would be a better place to live if the in-migration of permanent residents were somewhat limited. According to Wooden, the nonlocal: identifies with Western culture, feels only somewhat of an emotional attachment to Hawai'i, speaks Standard English, indicates a preference for Western foods, has a light complexion, has brown or blond hair, blames no one group for Hawai'i's problems, believes that women's roles are more diverse than just family-related, is a member of the middle-to-professional class and believes that control of immigration would not make Hawai'i a better place. One further distinction: the local is nonactivist, while the non-local gets politically involved.

Of course, Wooden's definitions are vast generalizations; within many residents, there is great variation in self-identification. However, a vital aspect of Wooden's definition is that "local" is quickly apparent. Even the most uninformed voter can assess a candidate's "localness" simply by seeing a photograph in the newspapers, a political advertisement on television, even by hearing a candidate's name or voice. Whether the voter acts on that assessment—ignoring political platforms in favor of superficial images—is less certain, but the potential for influence is obvious. As Franklin Odo observes about local identity, "Very frankly, this is our racism."

Scholar Jonathan Y. Okamura argues that a number of factors have contributed to the development of a local identity, but foremost among these are Japanese investment and tourism development, which will increasingly marginalize Hawai'i's people. "Continued affirmation of local identity over the past decade represents an expression of opposition to outside control and change of Hawaii and its land, peoples, and cultures," he says. Local identity is thus a group effort to maintain control of the economic and political future of Hawai'i against these outside forces. So strong is this identity that it may reduce emphasis on individual cultures to create a shared pan-ethnic identity. In this sense, it is based much more on *structural* factors than cultural.

At its most basic, local identity is about addressing feelings of powerlessness, according to Okamura. It is also an affirmation of "good" traits and manners of behavior, in contrast to "bad" traits adopted from whites and other immigrant groups. Scholar Eric Yamamoto explains that local identity is oriented toward values. "This approach to local as a value-orientation evolves from the conception of people's commitment to community and their acceptance of the related structure of interpersonal and business interactions," he says.

Local, of course, has its own language, Pidgin. "For some, Pidgin is the embodiment of modern Hawaii, a dialect weaned on social unity and class inequity, tolerance and xenophobic, pride and self-loathing," Michael Tsai writes in *Honolulu Weekly*. "For a growing number of others, however, it represents a general reluctance to accept the changes of the modern world." In essence, Pidgin excludes outsiders as it reinforces the shared heritage of local residents.

Like Pidgin, "local" is a distinction between "us" and "them." Eric Yamamoto explains that it is whites who are most often prejudged by local standards, not because of who they are, but because what whites do collectively is perceived as a threat to local people's self-determination. Jonathan Okamura concurs. "There is a clear danger of polarizing the Hawaii community between these two groups which could exacerbate ethnic tensions and hostility and expand social distance between groups," he says. However, Okamura adds that local also represents a coalescence of ethnic groups that can transcend differences. "Thus, the possibility exists that the concept of local may in the future come to represent all of the people of Hawaii."

Not everyone is so optimistic. "Somewhere, at some point in the kamaaina [Hawai'i born] coming of age, lies an insidious brand of elitism and racism so subtle that many Hawaii folks never see themselves as bigots," writes *Advertiser* columnist Esme M. Infante. "Celebrating local culture, we think we're open-minded and worldly. But the hypocrisy is that we tend to honor cultures of brown and black hair, not of blond. That local folks run to other local people first for help or friendship. That we shun those of foreign soil, even when their race is identical. That we assume people will behave in certain ways based solely on their skin color and whether they're Island-bred." Richard L. Rapson, too, is critical of localism, calling it a form of provincialism, which, though it exists everywhere in the world, is problematic. "Whenever the outsider is regarded as a threat and the local culture draws inward upon itself, ignorance, narrowness, isolation, and bigotry result," he says in *Fairly Lucky You Live Hawaii!* "I fear that localism, granting its virtues, is ultimately a malady, that the disease has progressed further in the islands than in most other places, and that it must be arrested before it becomes a malignancy."

On the campaign trail, ethnic appeals are kept subtle but are no less influential. In his self-published *The Akamai Strategist*, Hubert S. Kimura explains that the frequency of ethnic voting in Hawai'i is far greater than people have been led to believe, although he also notes that Japanese Americans do not necessarily vote so monolithically as some have argued. "Ethnicity is no longer the dominant issue for the younger AJA [American of Japanese Ancestry] politician," he says. They tend to see themselves as part of the larger local and international community. The fact that the sun is beginning to set on AJA political domination is less of a problem than what they consider more pressing issues." However, these changes do not mean that politicians should ignore ethnic groups. In fact, Kimura advises politicians to be concerned about the voting habits of many groups, particularly in terms of voter turnout.

"Some candidates have the ability to understand and appreciate various cultures in Hawaii," Kimura says. "The key, in my opinion, is to stress your candidate's respect and appreciation of the voter's cultural heritage and background. This strategy is not racism.... There is a clear and distinct difference between racism and an appeal for ethnic votes based on an appreciation of one's cultural background." Not surprisingly, Kimura also says that the "local factor" is important. He points to Honolulu's first prosecutor's race in modern times between Democrat Lee Spencer and Republican Charles Marsland, Jr., in 1980. Both men are white, but Spencer is from the mainland while Marsland was locally born and brought up. Marsland's use of his heritage in the campaign was central to his victory. "Localism is an emotional issue that has been used in numerous campaigns and will continue to be used in situations where local/non-local candidates clash," Kimura argues.

Though candidates continue to evoke localness in their campaigns, local identity is no guarantee of victory. Arnold Morgado, stressing "local roots, local values," finished second to Honolulu Mayor Jeremy Harris in the 1996 election for mayor. The race symbolized both the continuing battle between local (Morgado) and nonlocal (Harris) and factionalism in the state's Democratic Party, even though the mayor's race was nonpartisan. Morgado was backed by Governor Ben Cayetano, U.S. Senator Dan Inouye and First Hawaiian Bank's CEO Walter Dods, who wanted to head off a 1998 gubernatorial race between Cayetano and Harris. John Waihee and many of his former aides backed Harris, as did Frank Fasi's 1994 Best

Party lieutenant governor nominee, Danny Kaleikini. Harris countered Morgado's "local values" pitch with a more inclusive message of "shared values."

In that same election of 1996, David Arakawa won the nonpartisan primary for Honolulu city prosecutor by stressing his local roots. The descendant of a plantation store family, Arakawa used ads and signs that featured a *palaka* pattern evoking the plaid work shirts of the plantation era. Arakawa lost the general election to white mainland transplant Peter Carlisle, who stressed his experience and independence from the political establishment that largely endorsed Arakawa. The issue of ethnic heritage might have been a factor in the outcome of the 1996 city prosecutor's race. Arakawa supporters blamed election day rains that caused flooding and power outages for deterring Filipino-American and Japanese-American voters in certain rain-soaked neighborhoods—groups Arakawa appealed to—from turning out. "The haoles knew they had to vote," said one Japanese-American Arakawa supporter. Governor Cayetano extended the voting period on election day by one hour to accommodate voters, but some still complained of difficulties getting to the polls.

A nonlocal candidate can neutralize a local opponent by embracing local cultures. Such was the case in the 1st Congressional race between Neil Abercrombie and Orson Swindle in 1994. Abercrombie criticized his main opponent for not having lived long enough in Hawai'i to have "paid his dues." Swindle countered that the longest he had lived anywhere was six years in a Hanoi prison camp during the Vietnam War (Swindle, a Marine pilot, was a prisoner of war). Though he lost the election, Swindle managed to earn over 40 percent of the vote, suggesting that Abercrombie's criticism had little impact on the election's outcome. Though he managed to identify himself as the local candidate, Abercrombie himself was not born and reared in Hawai'i. In some ways, Neil Abercrombie personifies negative characteristics of whites— even his supporters agree that he is outspoken and aggressive.

Still, he has proven himself to be "locally sensitive," says Amefil Agbayani. "Swindle's not ours," says Agbayani. "He doesn't know what worries us. Abercrombie may be a loud-mouthed haole, but he is *our* loud-mouthed haole."

The *Haole* Experience

There has thus far been little written about "haole experience" in Hawai'i. As writer Judy Rohrer has explained, "Whiteness is a taboo subject, something white people do not talk about, much less explore and interrogate in print." But, says Rohrer, white privilege is at the center of what has happened to nonwhites in Hawai'i, especially the indigenous people. Whites or Caucasians as a whole are not considered an ethnic group, but rather a population based on broadly-defined social or folk concepts of race. As the largest continual immigrant group to Hawai'i, they will likely continue to be a prominent percentage of the state's population.

Haole is the Hawaiian word commonly used in the islands for a white person or Caucasian; it is both singular and plural ("haoles" is not a Hawaiian word, though it is commonly used). Island residents of Portuguese ancestry numbered about 14 percent of the population in 1890 and were counted as a separate ethnic group by Census takers. The U.S. Census officially abandoned the categories of Portuguese, Spanish and "Other Caucasians" in 1940. However, Portuguese are still considered a distinct ethnic group by many island residents and local demographers often count Portuguese residents separately.

Whites have been in Hawai'i for over 200 years, preceding all other groups in arrival, save Hawaiians. Many of the descendants of merchant and missionary families are rightly termed *kama'āina* (essentially "born of the land"). Intermarriage with other whites and especially Hawaiian *ali'i* produced close bonds among certain longtime resident families. Though relatively small in numbers, members of these families were closely connected to the ruling powers for much of Hawai'i's post-contact history. More recent white arrivals in Hawai'i are the military (some of whom remain after their tour of duty), young professionals fleeing the mainland for a change in experience (many of whom become connected with the University of Hawai'i) and other young people who come to pursue "alternative" lifestyles. There are also a number of retirees, many of them military or financially well off, who come to live their final years in the islands.

Recent white arrivals appear somewhat more sensitive to local customs than some of their predecessors, who were seen by residents as having imposed their values on others. "The Caucasian resident, as viewed by his local neighbors, is often automatically stereotyped as successful, independent, and self-confident," Thomas Maretzki and John McDermott report. "His aggressiveness, as perceived in business and interpersonal relations, results in such labels as 'loud-mouthed *haole*.' "

Whites are the most likely of all Hawai'i's people to congregate exclusively, and in the most expensive suburbs, in marked contrast to many nonwhites who have had limited choices regarding housing yet managed to live in ethnically-diverse neighborhoods. "Given the policy of ethnic separation and competition on the plantations, the ethnocentrism that can be expected among newcomers to a multi-ethnic setting, the international rivalries of the times, and the difficulties of securing a living on or off the plantations, there are good reasons for Hawaiians, Chinese, Japanese and Filipinos to have engaged in bitter conflicts," writes John Kirkpatrick. "That they largely did not do so is testimony to the positive effects of intermarriage, to traditions of tolerance, and to the ever-present reality of Haole domination." A careful observer of Hawai'i in the 1990s would also note the large number of impoverished whites living here. However, the *perception* that whites are successful is quite pervasive.

"The overall Haole population is, of all ethnic groups, least a single entity," explains Bernhard L. Hormann. "Except for the relatively few who are permanently identified with Hawaii, they are not unified. Their very diversity makes for movement and change." Many whites also have a difficult time getting along with others. How whites came to dominate Hawai'i politics and business is explained in part by racist ideology. "Although the theory of racial supremacy was probably believed by many haoles in Honolulu, for complex reasons unique to the Islands it never received legislative recognition, as in many mainland areas," according to Lawrence Fuchs. "Caucasian superiority could not be flaunted in the faces of Hawaiians, who after annexation had an overwhelming majority of the votes. Indeed, the haoles had in part built their power on the Hawaiian tradition of racial *aloha*. Haoles had accepted Hawaiian favors and Hawaiian daughters in marriage when, under the Kingdom, it was politically expedient; and the outward assertion of the *haole* racial supremacy would have been insulting to hapa-haole families." *Hapa*, meaning fragment, portion or half, is commonly used to refer to individuals of mixed race.

Whites' diversity makes it difficult to determine exactly what kind of candidate a local white voter might favor. Some argue that island whites are more inclined to vote Republican, though many are Democrats. That whites are prominent in Hawai'i's Republican Party, however, was quite evident in a full-page advertisement paid for by the Republican Party of Hawai'i featuring photographs and brief biographies of candidates for office in 1994. Of the 39 candidates shown, two-thirds were white. Like Democratic tickets, Republican tickets for governor have usually been ethnically balanced; for example, Hawaiian-Portuguese Andy Anderson headed the ticket twice in the 1980s, once with Japanese-American Pat Saiki and once with John Henry Felix, who is Portuguese (a group that often votes Republican). Despite this balance, both tickets lost, and the perception remains that Hawai'i Republicans are a party of whites. Many nonwhite residents also suspect whites of racial preference.

Whites continue to be major players in local politics, despite the demise of the white-Republican oligarchy in the 1950s and 1960s. Ironically, that demise was facilitated by other whites, notably labor leader Jack Hall and especially politician Jack Burns. Burns, a former policeman with blue-collar roots, served as governor from 1962 to 1974. To this day, he is spoken of reverentially by many islanders, especially second-generation Japanese Americans with whom Burns built the coalition that finally brought Democrats to power in 1954. *Honolulu Advertiser* columnist Samuel Crowningburg-Amalu wrote in his 1974 portrait of the former governor that one reason for the success of the mainland-born Burns among a diverse populace was that he had lived from an early age in working-class Kalihi. From this experience, Burns understood—as most other whites did not—that "there was something just a little bit wrong about the way that Island society was structured, something that violated the concepts upon which the American democracy was founded."

Burns had not been born into the island elite. He did not attend the islands' most prestigious private school, Punahou, and did not enroll at a prestigious Ivy League college. He did not wish to be a member of Honolulu's then all-white Pacific Club (which would eventually drop this racist membership requirement). He was known to pepper his private conversations with Pidgin. Burns was thus "local" and in touch with a majority of island residents. Crowningburg-Amalu credits him with bringing together as equals the two diverse elements of society—the descendants of big business and of plantation workers—in a bloodless revolution that resulted eventually in statehood. The late governor's popularity remains so high that even Republicans invoke his name when running for office.

Whites have held other high offices in recent decades. Four whites have been elected to the U.S. House, and one to the U.S. Senate. Oren Long, one of the last territorial governors, was elected to the Senate in 1959, but he retired after completing the term in 1962 (the term was shorter than the usual six years because Hawai'i had just become a state in

1959). Japanese-American Dan Inouye defeated Ben Dillingham, the son of white industrialist Walter Dillingham, for Long's seat, and has held it ever since. Tom Gill served briefly in the House in the early 1960s, but lost a 1964 Senate bid to incumbent Hiram Fong. Neil Abercrombie has represented the state's 1st Congressional District since 1990 and has often been challenged by other white candidates.

Orson Swindle challenged incumbent Neil Abercrombie again in 1996. Central issues in that campaign included which candidate possessed the "values" local voters find most compatible. "Hawaii is a special place," explained an Abercrombie television advertisement. "Orson Swindle just doesn't get it." Swindle appeared to have learned at least one crucial lesson about local politics, however: he made a bold attempt during the rematch to garner the essential Japanese-American vote by running newspaper advertisements that included endorsements of Swindle from some AJA World War II veterans. The move outraged Abercrombie, who has stressed his close affiliation with AJAs. It prompted other AJA veterans— in particular Hawai'i's senior U.S. Senator, Daniel Inouye, who lost his right arm fighting in Italy—to publicly announce their support of Abercombie. No *haole* has been elected either governor, lieutenant governor or U.S. Senator in the past quarter century. Whites have been candidates for all high offices, however, usually on Republican tickets. Whites are also well represented in the state Legislature and city and county councils.

The AJA Tradition

In his study of the 1970 Hawai'i governor's race, *Catch a Wave*, Tom Coffman details the manner in which ethnic heritage played a crucial role in that campaign. "Only afterward was it apparent that race and ethnicity had played such a large role, and that historic attachments proved to be so persistent, each racial group reacting in its own way to style, image, and issues," he says. "If not contrary to the Pacific

Golden Man mystique which is Hawaii's special halo, the ethnic undercurrents of the campaign reaffirmed the historic view of Hawaii as a series of immigrant waves, each contending for its place in the sun." In Coffman's book, it is Japanese Americans who find their place. Incumbent Democratic Governor Jack Burns was reelected despite a spirited primary challenge from his own lieutenant governor, Tom Gill. Burns was able to bring together the disparate elements of the Democratic Party— unions, the lower and middle classes and various ethnic groups—to gain office for the third time. He defeated Gill and crushed his Republican opponent, Samuel P. King (whose father, Samuel Wilder King, had been appointed the first part-Hawaiian governor of the territory in 1953), in the general election. So venerated was Burns, especially by Japanese, that he was occasionally, if ironically, called the "Great White Father."

It was the selection of Burns's running mate, state Senator George Ariyoshi, and Ariyoshi's subtle emphasizing of his ethnic origins that proved critical to the Democrats' victory. The lesson of the 1970 campaign was that to succeed in politics, 51 percent of the vote was not necessary, but a majority of the Japanese-American vote was. A Burns researcher told Coffman that Americans of Japanese ancestry comprised over 45 percent of the state's voting population at the time. Burns raised a six-figure sum from his political appointees alone. "The fund was called a *tanomoshi*, a Japanese word for an informal savings and loan," according to Coffman.

Hawai'i's Japanese Americans are the only island group to be commonly referred to by an acronym (AJA) and special names for generations (*issei* and *nisei* for first- and second-generation immigrants, respectively, as well as *sansei*, *yonsei* and *gosei*, which mean third-, fourth- and fifth-generation, but are used less often). University of Hawai'i Japanese-American scholar Dennis Ogawa explains, "Each generation has its own mentality, perceptions, values and experiences. There are certain intrinsic values that carry on, though, such as being community-minded, responsible to Hawai'i, concerned about education and family."

The term AJA emerged before and during World War II to distinguish Japanese Americans from Japanese nationals. While state Census figures show Japanese Americans are about one-fourth of the island population, in the 1990s more than half of the state Senate and about 40 percent of the state House came from this ethnic group. This is partly because Japanese descendants were for most of this century the single largest island group, but there are other, more complex reasons as well. "In essence the Japanese American living in Hawaii today, while middle-class in appearance, remains Japanese in heritage," observe Terence A. Rogers and Satoru Izutsu. Because the cultural base for Hawai'i's Japanese immigrants was rural, poor and conservative, they argue, Japanese-American society in modern Hawai'i can provide glimpses of nineteenth-century Japan. The good name of the family takes precedence over all personal considerations. Personal achievement is valued, and to bring shame on the family is the ultimate humiliation. The sense of obligation (*on*) had an important political impact on John Burns's eventually successful runs for governor. Burns had formed close relationships with the Japanese-American veterans who returned from their service during World War II with a new sense of purpose and identity that found its way into political expression. These *nisei* in highly decorated combat units earned respect for their bravery and patriotism at a time when 120,000 of their contemporaries were interned in U.S. concentration camps due to fear of possible collaboration with Japan.

Because the ethnically Japanese citizens have maintained their own identity and critical mass in Hawai'i, they have often influenced successive political campaigns, thus perpetuating their solidarity. Dennis M. Ogawa writes in *Kodomo no tame ni* of the ethnic cohesiveness that strongly influenced their post-World War II rise. "The family environment, community connections, and extensive obligations acted in concert to stimulate individual social mobility," he says. "The Nisei was interrelated with other Nisei in the common goal of success. When a Nisei declared *okage sama de* ('I am what I am because of you'), he was not just extending platitudinal gratitudes; he was expressing the dynamic core of Nisei's strategic cohesiveness—the interdependency of ethnic members in a common wealth of interest, goal, identity, and mobility."

Another Japanese-American scholar, Franklin S. Odo, cautions that the status of Japanese Americans in Hawai'i is not as monolithic or as harmonious as some believe, and that such views should be revised. "Indeed, it may be that such images, including alleged harmony or clannishness, which are the same quality given different values, are due to older interpretations of vertical structured relationships and the importance of group harmony imputed to Japan itself rather than observation of the ethnic group in Hawaii," he says.

Japanese descendants in Hawai'i do, however, have a highly-developed sense of their collective history as an immigrant group, says Odo—a quality of self-consciousness that began with the first immigrants. Among the objectives of contemporary Japanese are examining carefully their relationships with others—especially Hawaiians and whites, who are rising to more prominence because of demographic shifts—and being more aware of economic and political changes that increase the vulnerability of Japanese Americans who have become successful. Such debate must begin with AJAs themselves, Odo says.

Population trends point to more out-marriage and less cohesion among Japanese Americans in Hawai'i, but for now and the foreseeable future, they are the most critical group of Hawai'i voters. As voting statistician Bill Daly notes, they are more interested in politics as a group and more politically astute. Though their numbers, relative to all other ethnic groups, are slowly shrinking, they still participate in elections at a rate about 25 percent higher than their population alone would dictate. This is due to consistently high registration and turnout, according to Daly. "The AJAs are the only voting bloc in Hawai'i," he says.

Franklin Odo counters that Japanese-American participation in Hawai'i's electoral politics is a matter of participatory democracy, not ethnic domination. While acknowledging that heavy representation of Japanese surnames in the state Legislature, for example, fosters a continuance of this representation, Odo says Japanese Americans are under-represented in other arenas. "There are not many Japanese working in powerful positions down on Merchant Street (Honolulu's business district)," he points out. "The same is true for the University of Hawai'i, unless one includes secretaries."

Odo also believes that, as the financial status of Hawai'i's Japanese Americans improves, many are increasingly voting Republican—a pattern that is observable on the mainland as well. "Remember, it was a Democratic president, FDR, who signed Executive Order 9066 that put Japanese Americans into internment camps," Odo says of the pattern. "But there really weren't any camps here during World War II like there were on the mainland. Here, even though many Japanese are doing well financially, Republicans are still associated with the plantations."

Paul C. Phillips wrote in his study of Hawai'i's Democrats that George Ariyoshi was selected as Burns's 1970 running mate by a group of Democratic insiders. Ariyoshi was not their first pick, but when Hawai'i State Supreme Court Justice Bert Kobayashi rejected the offer, they turned to Ariyoshi, who accepted. He was selected not because he was highly regarded by insiders—he had had an unspectacular though steady career in the state Senate—but because they felt that Burns needed "an AJA on the ticket for racial balance." Nevertheless, a myth developed, created mostly by journalists, that Ariyoshi was the hand-picked successor of the so-called "Burns machine." Ariyoshi settled for a low-profile position in Burns's shadow until Burns fell ill in October 1973 and died the following year. Ariyoshi thus became governor and inheritor of the Burns mantle.

Tom Gill, who lost to Burns in the 1970 Democratic primary for governor, challenged Ariyoshi in 1974. Gill this time softened his image as a caustic wit with a sharp tongue and spoke of mellowing. He also emphasized that he was a *keiki 'o ka 'āina* ("child of the land"), or at least born in Hawai'i. Ariyoshi, meanwhile, had difficulties crafting an image other than that of a loyal Burns man. Longtime Honolulu mayor Frank Fasi also threw his hat into the ring, at one point attacking the advertising agency running Ariyoshi's campaign—and Ariyoshi by extension—because a member of that organization suggested that Fasi belonged to the Italian Mafia. Gill called Fasi a "Mussolini" at another point in the campaign, and Fasi countered that Gill was a racist. Another contretemps erupted when Bob Oshiro, long-time Democratic insider and organizer of Ariyoshi's 1974 campaign, wrote a speech to be delivered by another Burns man, Dan Aoki. Aoki had suffered discrimination on the plantations and remained bitter over the experience. A young Gill supporter, also of Japanese descent, heard Aoki's impassioned speech and suggested that it was a blatant appeal for race consciousness.

Near the end of the 1974 primary campaign, a part-Hawaiian former state school official named Daniel Akaka linked his bid for lieutenant governor to Ariyoshi's campaign for governor in an attempt to bring the Japanese and Hawaiian voters into the same camp. Instead, primary voters swept state Senator Nelson Doi into a pairing with Ariyoshi in the primary, the first time in history two Japanese Americans ran together for the state's top two positions. Their election also symbolized the continuance of the Burns machine after his death. "In 1974 the coalition which supported the Burns machine emerged clearly," Paul C. Phillips writes. "It was made up of those who had always stood at the peak of the economic and social pyramid, and those who had battled their way up in the last twenty years. They were the ins, the elites, the power-brokers, the establishment, and those who, for whatever reasons, saw their interests best protected by the status quo." This was accomplished despite heavy factionalism within the Democratic Party—and helped by the Republicans' failure to put together a credible alternative, Phillips argues.

In the four-way Democratic primary of 1974, Ariyoshi won 41 percent of the Japanese-American vote but only 13 percent of the white vote. In the general election, however, Ariyoshi led by a 5-to-1 margin among Japanese-American voters, while Republican opponent Randy Crossley led among whites by a 2-to-1 margin. In the 1978 gubernatorial election, Ariyoshi defeated Frank Fasi in the Democratic primary with a 3-to-1 margin of Japanese-American voters, though Fasi won the white vote by a 5-to-1 margin. In 1982, Ariyoshi won his third and final full term with 65 percent of the Japanese-American vote, though Republican opponent Andy Anderson won the white vote by a 2-to-1 margin over Ariyoshi. Third-party candidate Fasi was favored by 34 percent of white voters and a majority of Filipino-American voters, but had only 10 percent of the Japanese-American vote, according to an *Advertiser* story.

Ethnic Strategies

Gubernatorial elections are not the only ones in which race or ethnic identity matters—or at least seems to. During the 1970 U.S. Senate contest between Republican incumbent Hiram L. Fong and Democratic challenger Cec Heftel, according to Sidney M. Rosen, Fong used the issue of "local boy" versus "the mainland *haole*." One of Fong's paid advertisements noted that the Chinese-American senator was a "native son of Hawaii—*Keiki Hanau O Ka Aina*." Another time, Fong charged that Heftel did not know his constituents because he had not lived in Hawai'i long, Rosen says. Heftel's skin color was one reason that Hawai'i's other U.S. Senator, Democrat Dan Inouye, encouraged Heftel to run, as the state's white population was increasing. This angered Fong, who charged that Inouye was suggesting that there should not be two "Orientals" in the U.S. Senate and that it was time for Hawai'i to have a white representative. After Fong won reelection, he publicly refused to allow Inouye to escort him to the Senate's podium to take the oath of office, as Senate tradition dictated.

Though he retired from the Senate in 1977, Fong remains somewhat of an anomaly in Hawai'i politics: a successful Asian Republican. Many believe that Fong's political success was due more to his ties with labor unions, his personal character, and his Asian ancestry than true Republican colors, Daniel Tuttle reported in a 1966 collection of articles on Hawai'i elections.

Of all island population groups, the Chinese Americans have moved into island society the most completely. "The Chinese, more than any other immigrant group, had already acquired those characteristics which foreign observers think of as 'typically American,'" Lawrence W. Fuchs writes in *Hawaii Pono*. "Among second-generation Chinese, the English language, Christian religion, and American business and political methods had been energetically adopted. The transformation from the pig-tailed foreigner described by the Hawaii Board of Immigration to the full-fledged American of the 1930s represented the most successful adjustment of an immigrant group to life in Hawaii." The Chinese were the first to be brought in to work the plantations, but they were also the first to leave. They sought acceptance in Hawai'i and placed a premium on learning the English language and supporting the Christian churches. Politics provided an opportunity for status and influence. The Chinese were only 4.3 percent of registered voters in 1920, but that figure doubled by 1930. Prior to that time, a number of Chinese Hawaiians had been elected to territorial or county positions, usually receiving strong support from Chinese-ancestry voters. "The Chinese of Hawaii became known for their ability to get along with all groups," Fuchs writes. "For the most part, the Chinese failed to share the rising hostility of Hawaiians, haoles, and Portuguese for the Japanese. Chinese affability in part derived from the fact that the Japanese increasingly patronized Chinese businesses and professions and were a factor in the growing success of Chinese politicians." Though they make up only a small percentage of the island population, Hawai'i's Chinese Americans have a voter turnout rate second only to Japanese Americans—at over 80 percent of registered voters—according to vote counter Bill Daly.

Michaelyn Pi-hsia Chou wrote in her dissertation that Hiram Fong never played down his "Chineseness" while working with the predominately white elite and never forgot his family and friends. She maintained that this last characteristic proved to be one of Fong's strongest assets. She also dismissed accusations from Fong's early career that he had used his ancestry for political office. But ancestry was a factor. "When Fong ran for his first territorial senate race, every *pake* [slang for Chinese] in town of any worth worked hard for him," says Republican organizer Franklin Kometani.

Such has been the case many times over in the islands. In a 1970 study of a race for what was then Hawai'i's 12th Representative District (Waikīkī-Mō'ili'ili) in 1970, Allison H. Lynde observed David Hagino's first run for elective office. Hagino reasoned that he could count on fellow voters of Japanese ancestry, who comprised a majority of the residents of Mō'ili'ili. To that end, his campaign literature mailed to Mō'ili'ili neighborhoods featured endorsements by Japanese American politicians as well as several *haiku*, a traditional form of Japanese verse, suggesting that his election would bring forth positive change. Hagino used different mailings for Waikīkī, which had a mostly white population. These mailings emphasized his populist platform, with such slogans as "fair play for women," "Waikiki for the people," and "Put stadium land to good use," which appealed to liberal voters and supporters of then-Lieutenant Governor Tom Gill, who was challenging Governor Jack Burns in the Democratic primary.

The ethnic vote appeared to have been a factor in Hagino's gaining enough votes to run in the general election, Lynde said. He was the only Japanese American in a primary field of eleven. For the general election, Hagino arranged to have his Japanese middle name, Masato, included on the ballot, and again utilized select mailings to target voters.

Hagino's ethnic strategy failed in the 1970 general election, however. As Hawai'i representation was configured at the time, the top three vote-getters in an election district would represent that district in the state House. Lynde speculated that, despite his mailings and canvassing, Hagino received virtually no white vote in that general election and that he may have lost in part because of the emphasis on his Japanese ancestry. Indeed, the three winners of the general election were all white males, as was the fourth-place finisher. Lynde also noted that Hagino's age at the time (23), lack of name recognition and lack of campaign funds also contributed to his defeat. He would win the district eight years later.

Hubert Kimura observes in his self-published *Aikane-to-Aikane* ("friend to friend"), "There is no question that ethnic strategy plays a key role in Hawaii's elections." Kimura notes, however, that the relationship between a candidate's surname and a particular ethnic group is more complex than simple "ethnic voting" implies. Factors such as the cultural background of candidates and the manner in which ethnicity is handled during the campaign are important, but an "ethnic strategy" is a delicate matter and can backfire. Kimura believes that if a slate of candidates is predominantly of one ethnicity, voters tend to give their votes to a candidate who differs from the others. He advises politicians to concentrate on their own ethnic group as the most likely source of support, but also to attend and participate in ethnic events of others.

Scholar Michael Haas reported that all ethnic groups in Hawai'i display a degree of voting cohesion, though some groups have more electoral solidarity than others. Filipino and Japanese Americans vote more solidly, whites less so,

Hawaiians less solidly than whites and Chinese Americans less than all other groups. A 1980s study by the state lieutenant governor's office, which then oversaw all state elections, showed that "ethnicity is not destiny" in Hawai'i politics. The winner in 29 of 51 state House races in 1982 was not of the same ethnic background as the dominant group residing in each district. "Political success in Hawaii has something to do with ethnicity," the report concluded," but it has even more to do with a host of other issues...which in most elections in Hawaii either overwhelm the ethnic ties between the voter and the candidate or make it irrelevant."

But not always. In 1986, it appeared that John Waihee would be an also-ran to the well-financed gubernatorial campaign of U.S. Representative Cec Heftel. Waihee surprised everyone by beating Heftel for the Democratic nomination, pulling together a shaken Democratic Party and taking on the Republicans' strongest candidate in more than two decades, Andy Anderson. *Advertiser* political editor Jerry Burris recalls that, two days before the primary, a report about Cec Heftel's alleged drug usage was circulated among the media and prominent citizens in the community. Says Burris, the allegations were not reported in the media, though people wish to remember it that way in part because Heftel complained publicly after the election about a sexual smear campaign against him. Stories also circulated that Heftel was racist and anti-union—a matter that Burris does characterize as a smear campaign. Heftel eventually left Hawai'i for the mainland, but he remained active in politics, including fighting for campaign reform nationally.

"Waihee put together a strong coalition of native Hawaiian, Japanese-American and Filipino-American voters, plus vigorous support from organized labor and—despite a last-minute endorsement of Anderson from the Heftel camp—prevailed by 13,000 votes," according to *Honolulu* magazine. Waihee, who is three-quarters Hawaiian, attended school in Michigan and then returned to Hawai'i, graduating with the first class from the University of Hawai'i law school in 1976. Waihee came to public attention during the 1978 Constitutional Convention. Two years later he was elected to the state House from Kalihi Kai-Salt Lake. Reapportioned out of his district in 1982, Waihee took advantage of Lieutenant Governor Jean King's decision to run for governor and stepped into the lieutenant governor's race. Although he lost O'ahu, Waihee did well enough on the neighbor islands to edge veteran politico Dennis O'Connor by 4,000 votes. In his 1986 gubernatorial primary victory, Waihee took 19 out of the 20 representative districts where Japanese Americans were the largest voting group. Opponent Lee Heftel had a strong showing among Filipinos.

How important are the votes of particular groups? Bill Daly of Honolulu's Voter Contact Services says that voting patterns in gubernatorial elections are remarkably similar. The general "rule of thumb," he explains, is that 70 percent of registered whites, 90 percent of registered Japanese American, and 80 percent of other voter groups will vote in an election. This pattern has been consistent in Hawai'i elections. Voter Contact Services makes money and many candidates win office by making use of such information.

James C.F. Wang in *Hawaii State and Local Politics*, however, disputes the idea that various ethnic groups tend to vote as a "bloc." Nor can any politician "deliver" an ethnic group in a local election. Factors such as party allegiance and economic issues are more important in state and local politics than ethnic loyalties, he says. While there are examples of candidates who received a preponderance of votes from certain groups, Wang explains that, more often than not, such campaigns involve a candidate who was a longtime resident of the voting area. Bloc voting does not exist, Wang says, because ethnic groups do not agree on issues and candidates, groups are scattered throughout the state, each ethnic group is aware of the ramifications of asserting its own group too forcefully and all residents of the islands, regardless of ethnic origins, fall under the "spell" of tolerance and aloha. "There is a general feeling of repugnance towards anyone, politicians in particular, who openly makes an appeal on racial grounds," Wang observes. Race is a factor, he says, but only when an election is extremely close or when the candidates are relatively unknown.

Even when race is a consideration in a campaign, a candidate can miscalculate its role. Republican Pat Saiki, according to her adviser Andy Anderson, had a good chance of winning the governorship in 1994 because the state's population had expanded. The white voter population more nearly matched that of Japanese-American voters, who traditionally vote in large numbers for the Democratic gubernatorial candidate. As a Japanese American herself and as a politician with strong support among white voters, Saiki appeared to have a lock on the state's two largest ethnic groups. Saiki's campaign literature often illustrated her ethnic background. "I remember 1941 when I was a girl at the start of the war, when the soldiers in uniform came banging on our door," she is quoted as saying in one campaign brochure. "Since we were a family of Japanese ancestry, I was afraid. My family was not interned in the camps, but my uncle was...the experience moved me with a deep feeling inside to want to correct injustices done to others." A front-page story in the *Advertiser* recounted that experience as well. Jerry Burris termed the struggle between Saiki and Ben Cayetano for Japanese votes as a fight between "heritage and clan," meaning that Cayetano hoped Japanese would vote as they traditionally have—i.e., Democratic—while Saiki appealed to ethnic identity.

Early opinion polls seemed to indicate that Saiki did indeed appeal to both whites and Japanese Americans. A *Star-Bulletin* poll conducted statewide by Political/Media Research Inc. a year before the election showed that Saiki had support from 48 percent of Japanese-American voters and 46 percent of whites, twice the support drawn by Frank Fasi and Ben Cayetano, who would be her opponents in the 1994 general election. The three contenders split the Hawaiian and part-Hawaiian votes, but Saiki ran well behind Cayetano and well ahead of Fasi among Filipino-American voters. In February 1994, the same pollsters concluded that Saiki's support among whites, Japanese Americans and Hawaiians had increased further. Fasi's performance as Honolulu mayor was also evaluated by voters, showing that his tenure was approved by a majority of each of the four largest ethnic groups, but that he was not liked well enough to be governor and he had overstayed his welcome in local politics. A week before the November election, however, the *Advertiser* and Channel 2 News, using polls conducted by SMS Research, showed that Fasi now led among white voters, with Saiki second and Cayetano well behind. Cayetano had nearly half of all Japanese-American and Filipino-American support and one-third of Hawaiian support; Saiki led only among Chinese-American voters. Dan Boylan cautioned that Japanese preferences as polled were probably misleading. "Voters of Oriental ancestry do not tell anonymous telephone interrogators who they plan to vote for 12 months from now," he explained. By election day, Saiki's nearly state-wide support had dropped precipitously, while Fasi had emerged in less than a year to place second in the election and Cayetano had come from behind to win. It was Japanese-American support along with Filipino-American support that helped Cayetano most.

Though a Japanese American born and brought up in the islands, Saiki has been perceived by some to behave more like a white person, says campaign adviser Franklin Kometani. Indeed, most of Saiki's top advisers were white. A former school teacher, Saiki does not usually speak Pidgin in public. Her financial resources have allowed her to live in the wealthy and mostly white Honolulu neighborhood of Kāhala. Additionally, she has spent more of the past 20 years living on the mainland than in Hawai'i, and four of her five children live there. Of course, she is also a Republican. Saiki's 1994 campaign likely was also not aided much by the presence of Fred Hemmings.

Though locally born and brought up, and a former surfing champion, Hemmings is seen by many as a member of the white elite and as a political also-ran who has lost more races than he has won.

Saiki and Hemmings's experience may be taken to illustrate the role of socioeconomic class (money), as well as race/ethnicity (color), in Hawai'i elections. Their experience also illustrates that voter *perceptions* about money and color may carry more weight at the polls than the actual facts of a candidate's ancestry or net worth. This is as true in local elections as in gubernatorial contests. It is not always possible for candidates to manage the way they are seen by voters, however. For example, Susan Lai Young's 1994 campaign for the state House district that includes Honolulu's Chinatown had posters in both English and Chinese. Young lost. Honolulu City Council candidate Joe Pickard, a Kahuku native, aired a radio spot with two "local-sounding" voices to differentiate himself from incumbent Steve Holmes, an Iowa native of Irish ancestry, for O'ahu's North Shore seat. Pickard lost. Dennis M. Nakasato, a state Senator who challenged Neil Abercrombie in the primary that year for the 1st U.S. Congressional District seat, emphasized his extensive Japanese lineage in campaign literature. "Humble beginnings...sacrifices and hard work...your public servant," read one brochure, words to inspire not only Japanese Americans but other voters from similar backgrounds. Nakasato lost. City Council candidate Duke Bainum featured testimonials in his campaign brochures from local Japanese Americans. One compared Bainum's sincerity to "the resilient bamboo plant." Bainum won. John Mirikitani, a candidate for the Hawai'i Board of Education, emphasized the educational success of Japan as one reason why he should be elected. A Mirikitani advertisement in the local Japanese-American newspaper, the *Hawaii Herald*, stated "Domo Arigato (thank you very much)!" Mirikitani almost won. Though he finished among candidates for three at-large seats, he withdrew from the general election, citing health reasons, after he had came under public attack for exaggerations and distortions in his campaign literature.

Appeals to Japanese voters were most clearly evident in the 1994 gubernatorial campaign. On television, Frank Fasi noted that he had fought to get statehood for Hawai'i despite mainland prejudice against Japanese Americans, but added that people should not vote their ethnicity but instead vote for the candidate who has done the most to "level the playing field." A full-page ad for Pat Saiki read, "Honor and respect our beginnings." Nearly a dozen photographs of the candidate as a child dressed in traditional kimono and of her large family, including deceased relatives, illustrated the message. Republican Stan Koki's ads argued that a Saiki-Koki ticket would draw a wide variety of voters, meaning they would appeal to Japanese Americans and Okinawan Americans, both devoted voter constituencies. "Stan offers Pat Saiki the best chance to make real change," stated one ad. "Stan brings Saiki a strong multi-cultural voting base..."

The Democrats, however, were much more sophisticated in their appeal to Japanese-American voters. A four-page insert titled *"Shushin"* (Japanese for "moral and ethical values"), ran in the *Hawaii Herald*. "Some values know no ethnic boundaries," says the ad, which also lists other important examples of traditional Japanese behavior, such as *on gayashi* (to give back) and *oya koko* (to take care of one's parents). Ben Cayetano is pictured in the ad with his father, while another photograph features Cayetano with his daughter. Mazie Hirono is pictured with her mother. Testimonials from prominent local Japanese Americans decorate the back page. Inside, Cayetano's first run for the state House from a heavily AJA district, Pearl City, is recounted. Mazie Keiko Hirono's ("daughter of Laura Chie Hirono") "long journey" to high office is detailed, symbolizing the path of Hawai'i's Japanese immigrants moving out from "under the yoke of second-class citizenship" to eventual prominence.

Pat Saiki did manage to get a public endorsement from the family of Richard Matsuura, a respected politician who represented the Hilo area in the state Legislature. However, the family's endorsement of Saiki carried little weight, as Matsuura himself had appeared in Cayetano's 30-minute "Reach for the Moon" television message, praising the Democratic standard bearer. Maverick Frank Fasi, meanwhile, never did well with Japanese American voters, and 1994 was no exception. "Fasi does not have much in common with most AJAs," explains Bill Daly. "He is brash, outspoken, and anti-establishment. In short, he is very un-Japanese."

There are no special forums, festivals or newspapers specifically for appeals to white voters as there are for other groups in Hawai'i. In many ways, it is simply assumed that a white candidate will be popular among white voters. Local comedian Frank DeLima jokes about a fictional *haole* named Brad: "My name is Brad. Haoleness ran in my family. My mother was a haole, my father also. I live in the Waialae-Kahala district of Honolulu. I voted for Fred Hemmings in the last election."

Many white candidates have been transplanted mainlanders, a fact that has left them open to charges of misunderstanding local concerns and attitudes. After Jack Burns, who moved with his family from the mainland during his childhood, the most well-known white politician in the islands has been Fasi. Though a resident of Hawai'i for half a century, Fasi is an aggressive, arrogant and argumentative mainland-acting white man. Though he has continually received support from underprivileged Hawaiians and Filipino Americans, the only aspect of Fasi that is truly local is his use of the "shaka" sign during his many campaigns. Fasi is an intelligent man and an accomplished administrator, but he has never successfully mastered race politics in Hawai'i. His 1994 selection of running mate Danny Kaleikini—a wealthy entertainer with few connections to most Hawaiians—was widely seen as a flagrant attempt to win Hawaiian votes. The longtime mayor of Honolulu has rarely achieved strong support on the neighbor islands, and he has four failed attempts at the governorship to prove it. Most of Fasi's top advisers have also been white, including his former city managing director, Jeremy Harris.

Fasi first gained political notoriety in 1948, when he hired off-duty police officers to help his moving company carry featherbeds through Honolulu streets—a practice that landed him in court. Fasi's loss there inspired him to enter politics. "Fasi brought something new to Hawaii politics from the very beginning," Paul C. Phillips writes in his studies of Hawai'i's Democrats. "His aggressiveness—particularly toward fellow Democrats—far exceeded what was locally considered in good taste. He was acerbic. He was opportunistic, and he was a pragmatist. But most of all, in the provincial atmosphere of Hawaii politics in the 1950s, he was the malihini [outsider], and some Democrats were determined to set him apart."

Fasi first came to Hawai'i as a U.S. Marine during World War II. His family had immigrated from Sicily to Connecticut, and Fasi grew up in the slums of Hartford. He quit the Marines after the war, married a *nisei* woman from Kaua'i and went into business for himself, dealing in surplus materials. Like Jack Burns, Fasi suffered losses in his first runs for office. Early on, he had problems getting along with established Democratic leaders, but they backed him in a 1952 race against Democratic Honolulu Mayor Johnny Wilson for the position of national committeeman on the condition that Fasi would not challenge Wilson for the mayoralty. Fasi was elected to the committee position but then decided to run for mayor anyway (he explained it was "God's will" that he should run). That election also marked Fasi's first extensive use of newspaper advertising and radio appearances, a pattern that he would use in all of his political campaigns. The day and night before the 1952 election Fasi spent all 24 hours talking on the radio and taking phoned-in questions. He lost, and the victorious Wilson condemned the "malihini haole" who talked big.

Fasi spent the next two years campaigning, keeping himself in the public eye with a weekly radio show titled "Unreported

News," which he used to attack Wilson and other politicians, as well as the International Longshoremen's Warehousemen's Union (ILWU) and its leader, Robert McElrath. In 1954 Fasi separated himself from the Democrats and charged that the 80-year-old Wilson was too old to serve as mayor. Fasi defeated Wilson in the Democratic primary, but in the general election he lost to part-Hawaiian Neal Blaisdell, who, though Republican, had no ties to the Big Five. Bob Krauss, in his biography of Wilson, says that Democrats who were angry with Fasi were instrumental in electing a Republican mayor. Krauss also reports that Fasi spent over $5,000 in the primary campaign along with an additional $5,000 from Friends of Frank Fasi (a fund-raising organization). Wilson spent just $330.

Fasi continued to play politics and considered runs for other offices. He ran for the territorial Senate in 1958 but lost. He lost the general election for the U.S. Senate to Hiram Fong in 1959, and lost to Blaisdell again in the 1960 race for Honolulu mayor. He lost to Tom Gill in the race for one of Hawai'i's two U.S. Congress seats in 1962, but he was elected to the Honolulu City Council in 1964.

Fasi had by then established himself as a spokesman for the underdog, the poor and the disenchanted—a role that he would assume in all subsequent political campaigns. He opposed extensive development, putting himself at odds with the Burns faction of the Democratic party. In 1968 Fasi was finally elected mayor when he easily defeated Republican opponent Andy Anderson.

The Filipino Giant

No candidate has sought the Filipino-American vote more aggressively than Frank Fasi. "I look to the Filipino people," Fasi told the *Hawaii Filipino Chronicle*. "I know that the natural tendency is to vote for one of their own kind, but if they do, they are ingrates. There is nobody in an elected office today who has done as much to bring the Filipino people into the mainstream of the social, political and cultural life of this state as I have." It has been Fasi's particular habit to reach out to marginalized groups such as Filipino Americans. In a 1994 full-page advertisement in another Hawai'i newspaper, the *Fil-Am Courier*, Fasi explained that the "little guys," as he put it, had consistently voted for him. "It is not by chance that I have attended more Filipino functions over the years than probably all of the other gubernatorial candidates combined!" he declared. "Of my six office staff personnel, two are Filipinos," he noted. "I may not be Filipino, but I certainly am pro-Filipino. I know Filipinos want empowerment.... As governor, I would like to do for the Filipino community what Jack Burns did for the AJAs in the fifties." In a 1994 *Courier* cover story, written by "Friends of Frank F. Fasi," the authors noted Fasi had appointed Filipinos to 20 percent of all boards and commissions and they made up 20 percent of his department heads. "He changed the laws so Filipinos and other Asians could serve on the police force and in the fire department," they wrote. "No other politician has done as much as he has for the 'little guy,' regardless of race, religion or political party."

Hawai'i's first Filipino immigrants—fifteen men—reached O'ahu in 1906, and Filipino immigrants who followed were mostly male. A second wave of immigration, which included women, began after World War II, and a third—still ongoing—began after changes to U.S. immigration laws in 1965. Immigrant arrivals to Hawai'i in the 1990s numbered in the thousands annually, and most of these are from the Philippines, according to DBEDT statistics (net in-migration accounts for nearly half of island population growth). About three-fourths of all Filipinos in Hawai'i live on O'ahu, and about half on O'ahu live in just four areas: Kalihi-Pālama and Upper Kalihi near downtown Honolulu, and Waipahu and 'Ewa-Makakilo to the west of Honolulu, according to Eleanor Nordyke's *The Peopling of Hawaii*.

Bienvenido D. Junasa notes that Filipino Americans in Hawai'i have inherited the exaggerated negative stereotypes directed toward early immigrants. This has contributed to identity problems, even as they move into the mainstream of island society and focus on government and politics. "Although these achievements seem impressive against their plantation background, many Filipinos have felt that their political representation should be more nearly in accord with their number and talents in the community," Junasa says. Historically, explains UH ethnic studies professor Dean T. Alegado, emergence of solidarity among Filipinos is defensive in nature, arising as a reaction to perceived injustices committed against them by employers or those holding political power. "Filipinos do not express their ethnic solidarity simply because they share common occupations, but because they feel they have been long ignored and receive little attention from government," Alegado says. "Though less overt and intense, Filipinos continue to experience discrimination and anti-immigration chauvinism."

The chapter on Filipino Americans in Hawai'i's political history is slim, notes Dan Boylan. "Their numbers in elected ranks have been and remain few"; yet at the same time their prospects have never looked better. Attempts to woo the growing Filipino-American electorate have resulted in more appointed Filipino Americans in county and state government than ever before. The Filipino vote may be a "sleeping giant," Boylan adds.

Boylan has written that only a handful of Filipino Americans had a political impact in the first quarter of this century, but labor movements produced several key Filipino leaders during the plantation era. Because Filipino Americans today are congregated in just a few areas, however, their opportunity for political representation is great. Some in the community worry about factionalism, while others fear that Filipino Americans are more interested in voting for personalities than ideas. Amefil Agbayani, a political activist and UH staffer, says Filipino Americans are concerned about issues of discrimination, especially in employment. They will look beyond race should a candidate demonstrate support for Filipinos. Agbayani cited

state Representative Dennis Arakaki as a successful AJA
politician in a predominantly Filipino Honolulu neighborhood.
"He sings Filipino songs, he eats Filipino food," says Agbayani.
Bill Daly notes that, though Filipino Americans are the fastest
growing group in Hawai'i's population, their rate of political
participation is growing even faster. Despite this, they remain
about 20 percent under-registered given their relative numbers
within the island population.

Hawai'i's most prominent politician of Philippine ancestry,
Ben Cayetano, does not ignore the Filipino vote, but his
campaigns assume—correctly—that most Filipino Americans
will vote for a fellow Filipino. That does not mean the vote is
unsolicited. Cayetano was hounded by rumors during his first
run for lieutenant governor in 1986 that he had claimed he
did not need the Filipino-American vote. He said that his 1994
campaign for governor was one that Filipino Americans could
view with pride. Dan Boylan predicted, "Cayetano will get 80
percent of the Filipino vote, rock bottom, or I haven't lived
with a local Filipina [Boylan's wife] for the last 23 years." In a
1994 interview with the *Hawaii Filipino Chronicle*, Boylan said
that Filipinos who did not vote for Cayetano were "stupid," for
he was a highly-respected legislator who would do a great deal
for Filipinos.

Cayetano has not ignored other groups. In April of 1994,
sensing the significance of Hawaiian sovereignty movement,
Cayetano said that if elected governor he would return
Washington Place, the governor's mansion, to native
Hawaiians. He called the move a symbolic step toward
sovereignty. The mansion is where Hawai'i's last ruling
monarch, Queen Lili'uokalani, lived after the 1893 overthrow
of the monarchy; it was part of her estate when she died in
1917, and the territorial Legislature later purchased it (the
first governor to live in it was Republican Wallace Rider
Farrington in 1922). "I am not by blood a Hawaiian, but in my
heart—like many thousands who believe in the Hawaiian
people, I am Hawaiian, too," Cayetano said. Shortly after Ben

Cayetano's swearing in, the new governor—pressured by security concerns and also by the urging of traditionalists—decided to forgo his campaign pledge and moved into Washington Place. But, Cayetano has not ignored Hawaiian voters as governor. In 1997, for example, Cayetano ordered the body of popular Hawaiian entertainer Israel Kamakawiwoʻole to lie in state at the Capitol, though only politicians Jack Burns and Spark Matsunaga had previously been afforded such an honor.

But it is the Filipino vote that has been Cayetano's to lose. In 1978, he became the first Filipino American ever elected to the state Senate, where he gained a reputation for bucking the Democratic party hierarchy. He formed close friendships with several other independent-minded senators, including Charles Toguchi and Neil Abercrombie, all of whom were stripped of their committee chairs during a 1983 leadership struggle by then-Senate President Richard "Dickie" Wong. Cayetano's aversion to abuses of power began early. He left for Los Angeles in the 1960s after a Japanese-American supervisor gave a civil service job to another Japanese American, even though Cayetano had scored the highest grade on the civil service exam.

Cayetano has not overtly sought the Filipino-American vote, emphasizing whenever possible his belief that every vote is important. "I think the focus of the ethnic vote is a little too much, and it's something I would recommend that Filipinos need to get away from because they are not going to be able to elect any Filipinos if we are very parochial in our attitudes," he told *Mabuhay International Monitor*, a Hawaiʻi-based newsletter, in 1994. "We need to create candidates who are broadly accepted by the community at large." Cayetano also defends himself against charges that he has not given enough attention in his career to the needs of Filipinos. "I think that I have done my share," he said.

Other politicians have actively sought the Filipino-American vote. A *Chronicle* poll showed that Jeremy Harris led in the

1994 Honolulu mayoral race, but that Mito Ablan, a Filipino-American candidate, placed a strong second among Filipino-American voters, though he would finish back in the pack in the election. Ablan's full-page ads in the *Chronicle* stated, among other things, that "This is our only chance to elect our own to the office of the mayor. Now is the time! Vote for your own son, your own blood!" The Filipino vote was certainly critical at the mayoral race. Harris—a mainland transplant via Kaua'i who entered politics working for Frank Fasi in Honolulu—acknowledged their support in his victory, as supporters shouted, *"Mabuhay!"* (a Tagalog cheer) at his headquarters on election night. In a letter to the *Courier*, Harris thanked his supporters and promised open lines of communication with Filipino-American leaders who would advise him on Filipino matters, noting that he had previously declared August 13, 1994, "Filipino Community Center Day" in Honolulu—a declaration made just one month before the mayoral election. For a while, reporters credited Harris's wife, Ramona, for his victory, until it was later learned that she was not Filipino American but a mixture of several races and ethnicities.

Amefil Agbayani says the appointment of Filipino Americans to positions in government administrations is not cronyism, but rather "payback" for their support. She adds that such appointees are also qualified people—"Filipinos just want to be given a chance." UH-Mānoa Asian studies scholar Ricardo Trimillos says that Filipinos do not vote as uniformly as many suspect ("It depends on the situation") and that, even though a majority of Hawai'i's Filipino Americans did vote for Ben Cayetano in 1994, there was "lots of soul searching" involved in the process. This is because Cayetano is not considered "typically" Filipino. He does not usually associate with many other Filipino Americans or participate in Filipino organizations and functions. It was also a matter of embarrassment for devout Catholic Filipinos during the campaign that Cayetano was separated from his wife, says Trimillos.

To win high office in Hawai'i, a candidate must appeal to many ethnic groups. As the editors of one Filipino periodical observed, "The candidates' silence on this issue seems more like political expediency; their actions speak louder than their reticence. How else can you explain their omnipresence at Filipino functions?" It's not that each group—any group—votes uniformly. Every voter is an individual whose political decisions are influenced by many factors, which may include the ethnicity of the voter—or of the candidate. Nevertheless, each group is *perceived* to vote based on the appeal of candidates to ethnic sensibilities. As former journalist Peter Rosegg explained, "Ethnic voting is the 'little secret' that everyone in Hawaii politics knows about but few speak frankly about—at least, not publicly."

Hawaiian Kine

The most flagrant appeals for Hawaiian votes have come from Frank Fasi. Although required by law in recent years to choose its lieutenant governor candidate in a primary race, Fasi's Best Party in 1994 turned to Danny Kaleikini, hand-picked by Fasi to be his running mate. The decision startled many, as Kaleikini had no experience as a political candidate. Newspaper ads for the entertainer emphasized that Kaleikini "relates to all people—bridging the gap between nationalities and cultures," but it seemed clear that Fasi was more concerned about getting Hawaiian votes. "Hey, let me tell you, he's one smart Hawaiian," Fasi said of his running mate. He defended his choice by noting that other entertainers, such as Ronald Reagan, Sonny Bono and Clint Eastwood, had successfully run for elective office. He also chastised opponent Pat Saiki for having portrayed Dan Akaka, her 1990 Senate opponent, as a "dumb Hawaiian," a charge that Saiki denies.

Danny Kaleikini had been the headliner at O'ahu's Kahala Hilton (later sold and reopened as the Kahala Mandarin Oriental Hawaii), where he performed for 28 years, sharing Hawaiian music and culture with local audiences as well as wealthy tourists. "Aloha is so important, and when I see what's happening to Hawaii [it] just breaks my heart," he said shortly after the election. "People say you can't stop progress, *ae*, but there's a saying in Hawaiian, *mālama 'o ka 'āina*—you still have to take care of the land—and *mālama 'o ka 'ohana*, we have to remember to care for our families."

Kaleikini's commitments led to his involvement with Democratic campaigns from Jack Burns to John Waihee. But, he left that party to run with Fasi in 1994. "People are angry at conditions in Hawai'i, and anyone who thinks they can put sovereignty on the back burner has another guess coming because it's for real," he argued. "We must bring aloha back to government, we must bring aloha back to Hawai'i." During the campaign, Kaleikini wrote to a daily newspaper. The subject was sovereignty. "I intend to work for the return of all crown lands that were deeded over to the United States government by the illegally constituted Republic of Hawaii," he wrote. "I intend to make certain that the promise made by the Hawaiian Homes Commission Act, to make homestead lots and home sites available to Hawaiians, will become a reality." Like Fasi, however, Kaleikini stopped short of endorsing secession, explaining that he himself intended to remain "an American of Hawaiian ancestry." Kaleikini also made light of stereotypes of Hawaiians, claiming that his mother did not want him to run for office, telling him, "If anything goes wrong, everybody's going to blame you because you're Hawaiian."

In terms of political participation, Hawaiian numbers are considerably lower than those of whites and Asian Americans, though this was not always the case, especially in the first half of the twentieth century. Many Hawaiians were elected to the then-territorial government, a practice encouraged by the whites who held power. Politics provided the one aspect of life under the *haole* in which Hawaiians retained a sense of power, says Lawrence W. Fuchs. "The feeling was realistically based on the fact that the Hawaiians and part-Hawaiians constituted an absolute majority of the registered voters in the Islands for the first quarter of the twentieth century and the largest single voting group until 1940." Bob Stauffer noted in the *Honolulu Weekly* that by the 1920s and 1930s, Hawaiians had gained political power, office and influence never before held by a native people in the United States. "Hawaiians were local judges, attorneys, board and commission members, and nearly all of the civil service," he wrote. "This was 'democracy' in the classic sense: the spoils going to the electoral victors." Elected Hawaiians during this period were sympathetic to the interests of the pineapple and sugar industries, both controlled by white Republicans. James C.F. Wang marks 1962 and the election of Democratic Governor John A. Burns as the official demise of the oligarchy.

Many Hawaiians relished the power that enabled them to extract patronage, services and even cash payments from the whites who controlled Hawai'i during Republican rule, and a few believed that politics along racial lines might restore the islands to native control. "Widely used among the Hawaiian candidates was the slogan '*Nana i ka ili* ' (Look for the skin)," says Fuchs. It was the slogan for the Home Rule Party, led by Hawaiian radical Robert Wilcox, which dominated the first territorial Legislature at the turn of the last century. "But 'Look for the skin' was not a useful slogan for Hawaiian nationalists after Orientals began to vote," says Fuchs. "A large number of natives were always willing to join the haoles to defend against the alleged potential 'Oriental menace.'" Many Hawaiians also hedged in their relationships with whites. "Feeling that the ultimate destiny of the Hawaiian people was hopelessly predetermined, recognizing, perhaps incorrectly, that their own prestige, comfort, and immediate security depended upon haole largesse, they kept their deepest hostilities to themselves," according to Fuchs. Hawaiians' frustrations were later directed toward the Chinese and then especially toward the Japanese, who would greatly outnumber the Chinese.

"So race was the issue after all," wrote Gavan Daws. "King Kalākaua understood that as well as he understood anything.

His people had been dispossessed of their lands and they were being steadily disenfranchised by death, but while they lived they could vote, and if they all voted together they could make sure that Hawaiians sat in high places." This attitude led to the establishment of voting rights for citizens—Hawaiians and whites—but not Asians, a disenfranchisement that would continue well into the twentieth century. The federal Organic Act of 1900 effectively denied voting rights to the vast majority of Asians in the islands because of their failure to meet citizenship requirements.

Star-Bulletin journalist Ian Lind, who is part-Hawaiian, says that for the past 20 years Democrats have actively worked to recruit Hawaiians, whose numbers are growing, to replace the shrinking bloc of Japanese-American voters and keep Democrats in power. The Democrats' courting of Hawaiians is ironic for, as Lind explains, there is lingering resentment among Hawaiians after the Democrats' 1954 revolution because Japanese Americans replaced Hawaiians as the beneficiaries of government patronage.

Since the 1960s, Hawaiians have been elected to political offices, but not in numbers proportionate to their population. Republican Jimmy Kealoha served briefly as lieutenant governor in the 1960s. Democrat Daniel Akaka served in the U.S. House of Representatives and in 1990 was elected U.S. Senator, and reelected in 1996. Part-Hawaiian, part-Portuguese D.G. "Andy" Anderson ran unsuccessfully twice for Honolulu mayor and twice as the Republican nominee for governor. John Waihee served two terms as governor. His election as the nation's only governor of Hawaiian ancestry was a point of pride for many Hawaiians, though some have criticized Waihee for "selling out" Hawaiians to white and Japanese-American power brokers.

Cultural activist Henry Iwasa noted that Waihee traces his ancestry to Kamehameha I and was thus assured support from the *ali'i*, or ruling class, of contemporary Hawai'i. "Princess Abigail Kawananakoa, for example, wrote thousands of letters 'requesting' support for Waihee when he ran for governor," he said. Iwasa argued that Waihee was persuaded by the *ali'i* to be "more Hawaiian" while in office. Waihee's official state painting, for example, has him cloaked in a Hawaiian royal cape to signify his *ali'i* rank and show that he is not *maka'āinana* (a commoner). Iwasa explained that this is ironic given that Waihee played an active part in a movement which essentially sought to raise class consciousness as it endeavored for political gain. U.S. Senator Dan Akaka, presently the state's highest elected official of Hawaiian ancestry, is *maka'āinana*.

Jack Lewin, who served as Waihee's director of health for eight years, says Waihee was held to a higher standard because he was the state's first Hawaiian governor, a standard that Lewin believes was unrealistic. "He tried very, very hard to be fair, but he was still criticized," says Lewin. "He started his first term very well. He had a vision, a sense of direction. He was warm and congenial." By his second term, however, Hawai'i's economy began to change for the worse, and Waihee became a scapegoat because his administration spent too much money while expecting the state's 1980s financial boom to continue. "People only remember the bad things," says Lewin. "He doesn't get enough credit for the good things he did for Hawai'i. History will be kinder."

There are today Hawaiians at most levels of state and county government, and some wield considerable influence or are rising political stars, such as Republican Quentin Kuhio Kawananakoa, descendant of Prince David Kawananakoa and great nephew of Prince Jonah Kūhiō Kalaniana'ole (who was Hawai'i's Republican delegate to Congress from 1903 to 1921). He was elected to the state House in the 1994. Politicians like Kawananakoa—young, affluent, ethnic—excite local Republicans, but whether they help alter their party's image and lead to greater electoral victory is less clear. Democrats, meanwhile, have struggled to recruit promising young Hawaiian politicians and have been stung by high-profile controversy surrounding such senior Hawaiian party members as former

House speaker Henry Peters and Senate leader Richard "Dickie" Wong, who were appointed to the Bishop Estate Board of Trustees after their terms in office. Former House speaker Daniel Kihano was convicted in 1997 of campaign violations. In recent years, the presence of Native Hawaiians—or *kānaka maoli*—at the state Capitol has more often been found in overnight vigils by various Hawaiian organizations during legislative sessions to voice their support or opposition to pending legislation that directly affects Hawaiians.

Hawaiians have demonstrated political influence in less conventional ways, too. Shawn Kaui Hill, a television comedian and satirist better known by his stage name, Bu La'ia, registered to run in the Democratic primary for governor in 1994. Hill was only 28 years old at the time, two years short of eligibility for high elective office, so he registered using his older brother's driver's license. Hill officially withdrew from the race when accused by the Lieutenant Governor's Office of fraud, but he still earned over 5,000 votes in the primary, finishing third behind Ben Cayetano and Jack Lewin and ahead of four other candidates.

Hill's appeal was his position as a self-appointed champion of downtrodden Hawaiians, the Hawaiian "Supaman." The name "Bu La'ia" is a derivative of a local term, "bull liar" (Hill inserted a Hawaiian *okina* between the vowels so that his name reflected Hawaiian sensibilities, though it is not a Hawaiian name). To enhance his appeal, Hill donned a wig and blackened a front tooth. In local fashion, he wore a truncated T-shirt exposing his midsection, pulled his underwear up so that it was exposed above his waist and walked everywhere in his rubber slippers, cocking his head and smiling. Bu La'ia's statements during and after the campaign were thick with Pidgin. "I knew Cayetano was going win, cuz he get to count the vote. Cuz of he get Bu to count da votes, guaranteed Bu going win," he observed. "Every time da lieutenant governor win—Ariyoshi, Waihee, Cayetano. Next time going be da Japanese girl, Mazie."

His words, colored with local ethnic humor, resonated with many, making Bu La'ia a popular candidate. "When any injustice is done, I will help the underdog," he said. "I talk on da same level as da normal, everyday grovel-grovel sort of person." When asked why people should vote for him, Hill replied, "Cause I'm Hawaiian. Bu La'ia get plenty experience being one poor Hawaiian, welfare kine, no more money, gotta collect cans...groveling every day, fo' live in Hawaii nei." Observed Sue Villani in *Hawaii Investor*, "The proud country boy with the missing front tooth and wiry hair struck a nerve in the Hawaiian community. His comedy has a ring of truth to it, addressing such real-life issues as sovereignty, taxes, tourism, welfare and violence.... He's a hero to the local folks, endearing to everyone else." Hill's unsuccessful campaign apparently lifted him out of financial trouble. A few months after the election, he released a compact disc titled *False Crack???* in which he took pot shots at Cayetano and John Waihee while extolling Hawaiian dignity in such tracks as "No Mo Shame." More than 15,000 copies sold within a year. Demand for personal appearances pushed the price of a one-hour Bu La'ia gig from $250 to $2,000. A bumper sticker soon appeared that read: "No Blame Me, I Voted for Bu." Hill also authored a book on his comedic observations of island life and has said he may run for office again.

The Bu La'ia candidacy brought together issues of color and money (ethnicity and socioeconomic class), but it was not the first time this has happened in Hawai'i politics. David Hagino, for example, authored an unpublished document in the late 1970s titled "Palaka Power" for the cloth worn by many plantation hands and dock workers. "*Palaka* is a strong cloth," wrote Hagino. "It does not have the fragility or sheen of silk. It represents the strength of our people. We were strong enough to break the Big 5, to wage a bitter World War II, and to emerge from a depression.... *Palaka* is a cloth that has a fascinating, easing pattern of lines and colors. Its criss-cross pattern represents the interlocking strength of all our peoples to make one people and one culture."

Hagino wrote his manuscript for the nonprofit Hawaiian community organization Alu Like, but it served as a manifesto for the state's 1978 Constitutional Convention. Noting the decline of union power and the departure from the political arena veterans of the 1954 "revolution," Hagino proposed a new direction for the Democratic Party of Hawai'i, a direction that would continue to stress the egalitarian ideals of 1954 but also include the voices of other people in Hawai'i who were under-represented. He noted the rise of a socioeconomic elite comprised mostly of educated whites and Asians. "Palaka power" would presumably include the voices of others. "Palaka power" as a concept has faded, but its populist, ethnic appeal is still palpable, though many question its true purpose. Jerry Burris, for one, believes "palaka power" is just another name for cronyism, as he argued in *The Price of Paradise: Volume II*. Hagino acknowledged that some people thought that "Palaka Power" was racist, a "them against us" tract, but Hagino viewed it instead as a way to include in the political process voices from groups that have thus far been ignored. As the Bu La'ia candidacy of 1994 demonstrated, the issues Hagino raised 20 years earlier remain powerful—and unresolved.

A Sovereign Land

The most visible Hawaiian leaders of recent years have emerged from neither of the major political parties, but from the Hawaiian sovereignty movement. The origins of this movement date from the early 1970s, when the development of O'ahu's Kalama Valley was opposed by residents, many of them Hawaiian. That incident sparked an ongoing series of land struggles that continue through the present day, though the nature of the protests has changed. "Land claims first appeared, as in Kalama Valley, as community-based assertions for the preservation of agricultural land against resort and subdivision use," explained UH Hawaiian studies scholar Haunani-Kay Trask. "By the mid 1970s, these claims had broadened to cover military-controlled lands and trust lands specifically set aside for Hawaiians by the U.S. Congress but used by non-beneficiaries."

Another prominent struggle was carried on by the Protect Kahoʻolawe Ohana, organized to stop the military bombing of the unpopulated island near Maui. Ancient chants refer to the island as a landmark on ancient Polynesian voyaging routes. It also has many culturally-important archaeological sites. Hawaiian activists George Helm and James "Kimo" Mitchell disappeared and were presumed dead during a 1977 ocean crossing to protest the bombing and today are remembered as martyrs to the cause. In the 1990s, the Ohana succeeded in its efforts, and Kahoʻolawe was designated a national historic site. Religious worship has also been revived there as the U.S. military has worked to clean up the damaged island.

Hawaiian studies—where students are introduced to Hawaiian history, culture and politics—and language classes at the University of Hawaiʻi have flourished in recent years, as have Hawaiian language immersion programs in some elementary and secondary schools. In May 1997, for the first time, a majority of those elected to lead the Associated Students of the University of Hawaiʻi—the university's student government—were Hawaiian studies students, who took advantage of chronic student-voter apathy to get elected on a Native Hawaiian slate. The last quarter of the twentieth century has seen a resurgence of Hawaiian culture and Hawaiian pride, which might foster more political success. Perhaps most critically, several prominent sovereignty groups emerged in the 1980s and 1990s, including the state-supported sovereignty department, the Office of Hawaiian Affairs (OHA), and the largest independent island sovereignty group, Ka Lāhui. The aims of these groups vary, but what is shared is a desire to achieve some form of Hawaiian autonomy.

Wendy Kaleiwahea and Malia Kahale of Honolulu-based Voter Contact Services note that as of the mid-1990s, there were nearly 60,000 Native Hawaiian voters registered with the Office of Hawaiian Affairs. They represent 14.3 percent of all voters in Hawai'i and live in every area of the state. Every state representative district contains more than 5 percent OHA voters.

While Hawai'i's future in terms of race and ethnicity in local politics is unclear, it is likely that increased Hawaiian nationalism and the sovereignty movement will play a major—perhaps critical—role. As public opinion polls reflect, only a minority of residents feel that Native Hawaiians should not be compensated in some fashion for the overthrow of the Hawaiian Nation. Only the manner of redress is disputed. Calls for sovereignty reached a peak in January of 1993, the 100th anniversary of the overthrow of the Hawaiian monarchy. Haunani-Kay Trask argued that the American presence in Hawai'i should be considered as unwanted colonization—a point that is not well understood by Hawaiians because America has presented itself as a force of anti-colonialism. Trask writes that Hawaiians have gradually begun to discover the consequences of American occupation, which has repressed the Hawaiian people and their culture. This is leading to a rejection of Americanization. Land and water—including problems of governmental encroachment and legal rights, cultural expression, which includes the teaching of Hawaiian religion and principles of protecting the land, and community services, especially health and education—are at the forefront of Hawaiian concerns, explained Trask. The state government's Office of Hawaiian Affairs (OHA) is inadequate to the task of helping Hawaiians and is, in fact, an obstacle to self-determination (although Trask's sister, Mililani, has considered running for the board herself).

At present, the sovereignty movement is divided among several factions. One of the largest and most powerful of these is OHA, the state-supported, semi-autonomous Hawaiian affairs office. OHA seeks a plebiscite to determine the best model for sovereignty, though a state-within-a-state model as a possible step toward a nation-within-a-nation model is supported by many OHA leaders. Ka Lāhui, the largest sovereignty group, seeks nation-within-a-nation status without the direct involvement of non-Hawaiians and the state. Several smaller organizations vary considerably in the means they seek to achieve sovereignty but share similar goals. There is often bitter disagreement among these factions, leading some observers to question whether Hawaiians will ever be able to agree on sovereignty, let alone a model. Then again, perhaps that disagreement is simply a necessary part of the process. Mahealani Kamauu and H. K. Bruss Keppeler, in a Ka Lāhui publication, write: "The advantage of living in a democratic society is that people can embrace their own ideals. The Hawaiian community is moving ahead with sovereignty through its discussions and even through its differences. Some might call this 'infighting,' but remember that disagreement occurs only when you have commitment to an issue—people fight for things worth fighting for. No ethnic group agrees on everything—Hawaiians are no different."

Kekuni Blaisdell, who heads one of the smaller sovereignty factions, Ka Pākaukau, argues that cultural pluralism with its promise of equal opportunity has not met the needs of Hawaiians, who were forced to adopt Western ways. A physician, Blaisdell is particularly concerned with what such habits have done to the health of Hawaiians, who have suffered greatly under a diet of excessive saturated fat, sugar and salt. Ka Pākaukau, Ka Lāhui and OHA each seek to advance Hawaiian interests. Among the issues most pressing are reparations for the 1893 overthrow, legal claims to ceded Hawaiian Homes and other trust lands abused by the state and federal governments and by large private trust estates, and United Nations recognition of aboriginal land rights. These matters are no longer ignored by non-Hawaiians, especially reparations and land claims. "Hawaiians may not own the assets of Hawaii, but they are the backbone of the state's economy and they are its spirit and its soul," Blaisdell said in an *Advertiser* story, adding that Hawaiians have power but have not used it. "If native Hawaiians did not go to work tomorrow, the state of Hawaii could not function."

David Hagino notes that there are "tons of money" in parts of the Hawaiian community, such as the Bishop Estate, the Lili'uokalani Trust, the Department of Hawaiian Home Lands and OHA. "What they got to do is distribute it equally. If you totaled all of these assets, [which amount to] something like $40 billion, Hawaiians would probably be the richest ethnic group in the world." Sovereignty will not elevate the status of Hawaiians, argues Hagino. "Sovereignty plus poverty equals poverty."

For many in Hawai'i, the consensus seems to be a lukewarm support of sovereignty, although this position may be more one of self-interest than sincere concern to see that justice is done. Not surprisingly, some have already suggested ways to make sovereignty profitable. "Although the Chamber of Commerce here in Hawaii remains somewhat apprehensive about sovereignty, both the Hawaii Hotel Association and the Hawaii Visitors Bureau claim to be sovereignty supporters who view the creation of a Hawaiian nation as economically beneficially," observed Ian Hodges in a *Weekly* article. "In the interests of its own economic survival, Hawaii's business community is beginning to learn about sovereignty. From a purely economic point of view, supporting the creation of a sovereign nation is a strategy that is certainly preferable to jailing the movement's leaders." A widely shared concern among non-Hawaiians is, "How will sovereignty affect me?" Responses from sovereignty groups vary, but most make assurances that non-Hawaiians will be accommodated in a new Hawaiian nation. But, that promise does not satisfy all island residents.

What most observers would probably acknowledge but few have said publicly is that sovereignty is, at its most basic, about power. The possibility that those who hold power may have to give it up is unsettling. "Right now there's a lot of hypocritical lip service to sovereignty in the general community, including among politicians," wrote former *Advertiser* editor John Griffin. "Yet there are also a lot of people, Asian-Americans and haoles, who have a vested interest in the post-colonial setup we have today. Many may not like sharing." But many want to share in other matters, starting with the serious issue of whether non-Hawaiians should have a say about sovereignty, since, they point out, its consequences affect all island residents.

Others believe sovereignty will bring trouble if it necessitates the taking of property. "As soon as you take one acre or one tenth [of property] from a Japanese or a *haole*, the shit will hit the fan," says Richard Rapson. "Hawaiian sovereignty is a time bomb; it is a class revolt, because most Hawaiians are poor and have no association with Hawaiian royalty or intellectuals. Most Hawaiians want education for their kids, a home of their own; they aspire to the middle class. Western society is very appealing to Hawaiians, but sovereignty is not headed in that direction."

"A silent majority of Hawaiians don't want sovereignty," according to Henry Iwasa. "For one thing, there's been too much mixture of the Hawaiian people." However, Iwasa believes that an independent nation would actually help Hawai'i's multicultural society. "Distinctive Hawaiian values could pervade where American values have failed," he says. "*Aloha* is overused, but *pono* [excellence, prosperity, righteousness], *lokahi* [unity, agreement, harmony], the *'āina*, these have almost mystical qualities. If they would be allowed to flourish rather than be circumvented, that will foster tolerance and openness. Culturally speaking, this could not take place in Iowa or Mississippi." Iwasa notes that nineteenth-century Hawaiian culture was rich and literate and included a sharing of American and Hawaiian cultures, because it was recognized that the integration of foreign influence could have positive benefits. "Most people in the sovereignty movement are not aware of this or have forgotten this," he says, in part because some of these activists are too influenced by radical civil rights movements outside Hawai'i. "I'd like to see these old Hawaiian values continue, to be resurrected, to have the re-Hawaiianization of Hawai'i."

It is possible that the best chance for sovereignty may arise out of the serious decline in Hawai'i's economy at the century's close. UH-Mānoa futurist James Dator, in a *Star-Bulletin* story, predicted that sovereignty will emerge as the state's number-one issue in the next century and, therefore, the Hawaiian community will grow in importance, though that community will remain divided. He also foresaw a Hawai'i with little control over its own destiny, largely controlled and owned by outsiders. Others, however, believe that the islands have the resources and energy to turn their direction into a more prosperous future, one less reliant on tourism, with more investment in education, small business, retailing, banking and diversified agriculture. All could be accomplished under a sovereign government.

The continuing sovereignty discussion may provide the lens to focus a variety of social and economic issues that trouble Hawai'i as the century comes to a close. As sovereignty leaders pursue the economic as well as the political empowerment of Native Hawaiians, they can inspire others to embrace Hawaiian values. Instead of following the model presupposed by Jack Burns's warning—that one large and powerful ethnic group would exploit the rest of the population if it only could—Hawai'i's sovereignty movement may yet educate the nation and the world about caring, justice, sharing and the preservation of increasingly scarce resources.

SEX: "THREE STEPS BEHIND"

HAWAI'I IS ONE of only a handful of states with a female represent-ative in the U.S. Congress. Though it is the youngest of the fifty states, it sent a woman to Congress ahead of 20 others. The state Constitution prohibits discrimination on the basis of sex, and Hawai'i was the first state to ratify the Equal Rights Amendment to the U.S. Constitution.

It was not the first time the islands had demonstrated progressive thinking in terms of women's rights. A bill for women's suffrage in Hawai'i was introduced by the territorial delegate to Congress, Prince Jonah Kūhiō, in 1914, and the territorial Senate passed the Hawaii Equal Suffrage Bill in 1917. In 1919 the territorial House Judiciary Committee unanimously passed a women's suffrage bill for the islands. In 1970 Hawai'i became the first state to give women access to safe, legal abortions. Two women have served as lieutenant governor and one as mayor of the state's largest city and county, Honolulu. Several women have been mayors of the smaller counties. Such observations lead easily to the conclusion that Hawai'i is "friendly" to women, that women here enjoy a measure of equality and political power that eludes their sisters elsewhere.

Still, women's roles in Hawai'i politics and the overall socioeconomic status of females is considerably smaller than men's. Martha Ross, a director of the Hawaii State Commission on the Status of Women, says that progress for women has been slow, particularly in certain fields. There has also been a backlash against women's progress in recent years. "Women don't have a fifty-fifty chance of being governor or going to Congress," she says. "When men and women are paid equally, when the rates of domestic violence are reduced, we can then say there is equity between the sexes."

All of Hawai'i's governors have been male. Jean King served one term as lieutenant governor under George Ariyoshi and, after an unsuccessful challenge for his job in 1982, disappeared from local politics. The Republican tickets of Andy Anderson and Pat Saiki in 1982 and Fred Hemmings and Billie Beamer in 1990 (Beamer also ran for the same spot as a Democrat in 1978) suggest that women are increasingly being taken seriously as candidates for high office; yet, in both of these campaigns, males still headed the ticket. Both tickets also lost. Male dominance is evident in other political arenas as well. Hawai'i's Legislature, mayoralships and city and county councils have largely been the domain of male politicians. Democrat Eileen Anderson upset incumbent Frank Fasi in the 1980 Honolulu mayoral primary and was elected mayor in the general election, but she lost to Fasi four years later (Fasi, at the urging of Republican Andy Anderson, had switched to the Republican Party). Like Jean King, Eileen Anderson subsequently disappeared from politics. "Jean King was a lightweight," former state Senator Mary George says. "And Eileen was a lousy mayor. I think women have done well in politics, and the situation is improving."

Profiles in Power

According to DBEDT, on average some 60 percent of eligible citizens are registered to vote in Hawai'i, and females lead males by about five percent. Of those who do vote, females lead males by about three percent. From 1972 to 1992, females outvoted men by 10,000 to 20,000 per election. But, high numbers of voters do not mean women are more politically active than men. Coralie Chun Matayoshi observed in a study by the Center for Women in Government that Hawai'i women had the nation's lowest participation rate in senior state and local government posts, at just below 15 percent. This is contrasted with the fact that Hawai'i has at times led the nation in the number of women holding elective office at the state and county level.

Progress takes times, of course. From 1959 to 1973, there were from two to four women serving in the state Legislature, and in 1974—the height of the women's movement—that number doubled. Women increased to 14 percent of the Legislature in 1980 and 17 percent in 1982. Nationally at this time, women held only 13 percent of all state legislative seats (Eileen Anderson was elected Honolulu mayor at a time when women represented only eight percent of U.S. mayors). Jean King served in the state Legislature from 1972 until 1978, when she won the lieutenant governorship, a position she held for one four-year term until she lost in the Democratic primary for governor. While she was lieutenant governor, King was one of only ten women nationwide to serve in that capacity.

Since 1980, women have served increasingly on city and county councils. Women occupied 27 percent of all council seats in 1980, a figure considerably higher than the nationwide average of 10 percent. Those council members followed in the footsteps of some groundbreaking women. Marilyn Bornhorst was the first woman elected chair of the Honolulu City Council, in 1968. Betty Vitousek was the first woman to serve as a district court judge in the islands, in 1961. Rhoda Lewis was the first woman justice of the five-member state Supreme

Court, serving from 1959 to 1967. Paula Nakayama, who joined the court in 1991, is the second. Ah Quon McElrath, widow of the late labor activist Robert McElrath, is arguably the best-known woman in Hawai'i labor history. She currently is a member of the University of Hawai'i Board of Regents. In 1996, Governor Cayetano named Lily Yao, president and chief executive officer of Pioneer Federal Savings Bank, to that board.

The county of Kaua'i has had two female mayors: Mayor Jo Ann Yukimura was defeated for her bid for reelection in 1994's Democratic primary, but Republican Maryanne Kusaka was elected to the position in the general election. On Maui, Linda Lingle was reelected as mayor in 1994. Hawai'i county elected Helene Hale in 1962 (the first African-American woman mayor in the U.S.) and Lorraine Inouye in the early 1990s (the first Filipino-American woman mayor in the U.S.). Pat Saiki and Patsy Mink have served in the U.S. House of Representatives, though both have failed in attempts for more powerful positions in the U.S. Senate and the Hawai'i governor's office.

Linda Lingle, a Republican candidate for governor in 1998, hoped to break that pattern in November 1998, but had already come under attack before she officially declared whether she would run. "She's anti-union," some protested upon hearing Lingle's plans to privatize certain government services—even though Lingle had worked for Maui's Teamsters. *MidWeek* columnist Eddie Sherman passed along salacious rumors about Lingle, adding that none of them were true. That such "rumors" would even surface, however, says a great deal about Hawai'i's attitude toward female leaders. However, other personal characteristics of Lingle—she is Jewish, from the mainland, lives on Maui, is twice-divorced and childless—could affect her candidacy in a state that upholds "family values" and tradition and usually favors the local-born and O'ahu-based.

Despite women's secondary status, their votes are highly valued by candidates and campaigns for elective office, because women are more likely than men to vote, although there are actually several thousand more males than females living in Hawai'i. Eleanor C. Nordyke explains in *The Peopling of Hawaii* that the sex ratio has historically favored males. Additionally, the presence of military personnel means there are about 15 percent more men than women in the 20- to 24-year-old category. For persons 75 and over, however, the ratio runs in the opposite direction, or about 80 males per 100 females—a ratio that exceeds the U.S. average.

As on the mainland, women in Hawai'i live longer than men. The median age of all people in Hawai'i in the 1990s was about 33 years; life expectancy for males was just over 75 years and 80 years for females, according to Department of Business, Economic Development and Tourism (DBEDT) statistics. Nordyke notes that Chinese females have the greatest longevity (82 years) and Hawaiian males the shortest (71), based on 1980 statistics. Nordyke also notes a gradually aging trend in the islands, though Hawai'i's people are younger overall than those in most of the United States. Hawai'i betters the national rate for many key indicators on vital health statistics. Infant mortality remains below the national level. Lung cancer is the leading cause of cancer deaths for men and women, but is well under the nation's lung cancer death rate. Hawai'i's female breast cancer death rate is also below the nation's (it is the second leading cause of cancer deaths among women), according to the state Department of Health (DOH).

Health and welfare statistics reveal a great deal about the power women have in a society. In Hawai'i they reveal that women's well-being is not a paramount concern of the society or its elected officials. Over 2,500 Hawai'i families are homeless, or one out of 100. Some 16,000 families live in poverty. Almost 42,000 children under the age of 18 live with single parents. Nearly 700 babies are born annually to mothers 17 years and younger (the age of sexual consent for Hawai'i is 14, two years earlier than it is in most other states). Over 1,500 children are in state care due to their own or family problems, according to the "1995 Hawaii Kids Count Data Book." One source estimates that over 2,600 people are victims of domestic violence each year in Honolulu alone. The rate of child abuse and neglect for children under five doubled from 1980 to 1990, with sexual abuse as a major factor. Girls are more likely to be victims than boys, and girls are two to five times more likely than boys to suffer from incest or third-party sexual abuse.

According to the Domestic Violence Intervention Program, which is funded by the state's Department of Human Services (DHS), domestic violence is: "A pattern of controlling behavior which can involve physical, sexual, economic, emotional, and psychological abuse." It affects people in all social, economic, racial, religious and ethnic groups, whether people are married, divorced, living together, dating or in a gay or lesbian relationship. Women, however, are by far the most common victims.

The FBI estimates that half of all women nationally will be physically abused at some point in their lives by men with whom they live; the U.S. Surgeon General reports that battering is the single most common cause of injury to women, resulting in more injuries than auto accidents, rapes and muggings combined. Annually in the United States, more than one million abused women seek medical help for injuries caused by battering, while two to four million American women of all races are beaten annually by their partners. It is estimated that a woman is severely beaten every 18 seconds, six million women are severely beaten annually and nearly 2,000 will die as a direct result of battering every year. Rape is also a significant or major form of abuse in 54 percent of violent marriages.

These national statistics apply to Hawai'i. *MidWeek* newspaper reported in 1998 that Hawai'i women were following another mainland trend—record numbers of women were purchasing guns, despite state regulations that prohibit the carrying of firearms. Fundamental changes in attitudes toward women and violence in Hawai'i may be very difficult to change because they are so deeply rooted—physically, as well as psychologically. Phyllis Turnbull and Kathy E. Ferguson have written that a key reason why Hawai'i oppresses women is the large presence of the U.S. military, who, following the lead of Christian missionaries, "colonized" the islands as masculine invaders of a "soft," feminine locale.

A climate of domestic abuse cannot be ignored in a discussion of women's experiences in politics. Abuse is the abuser's attempt to gain power and control over the victim, say researchers. It is a learned behavior, not caused by mental illness, bad temper, stress, or drugs or alcohol. It escalates over time in both frequency and severity, and it will not stop without specialized intervention and treatment.

Unfortunately, there is a serious backlog of domestic violence jury trials in Hawai'i. A report by the state Center for Alternative Dispute Resolution recommended to the state Legislature as recently as 1993 a number of steps to ease this backlog, and the House established a Domestic Violence Coordinating Council to address the issue of family court jury trial backlog and adverse consequences for victims of domestic violence. Researchers Pamela Ferguson-Brey and Jodi Nishioka dispel the myths that men commit spousal abuse in equal numbers and intensity as women. "When compared to men, women annually experience over ten times as many incidents of violence by an intimate," they reported in an *Advertiser* story. The Hawaii State Commission on the Status of Women reported that in 1993 the minimum percentage of victims of domestic abuse in Hawai'i was 14 percent; when the average percentage of people who keep such matters private is factored in, the abuse rate is estimated to be 20 percent. "In numbers, over 49,000 women in the state of Hawaii between the ages of 18 and 64 are victims of domestic violence," the Commission concluded. A "typical" victim was between the ages of 20 and 40, either formerly or currently intimate (married or a partner) with their abuser, and white or Hawaiian.

Martha Ross cites several reports that suggest the abuse rate of women aged 18 to 65 is closer to 25 percent. The degree of domestic violence ranges from verbal harassment to threats of physical violence, from date rape to murder. Domestic violence cuts across all racial-ethnic and socioeconomic lines in Hawai'i. There is only a difference in the percentages of people who report such incidents. Asian groups in particular, but also Pacific Islanders, are reluctant for cultural reasons to report domestic violence due to fear of shame or rejection, according to Ross. Higher percentages of reports of domestic violence tend to come from lower-income groups, which is probably due to the housing proximity of friends and neighbors who call the police. Additionally, upper-income individuals have more resources than those from lower-income groups and thus are less likely to turn up at domestic violence shelters. Ross explains that domestic violence is not limited to heterosexual couples, although it is much more prominent among these couples. There are also incidents of women inflicting violence on men.

"As long as an individual buys into power [concepts], the potential for violence is there," Ross says, adding that violence is ingrained in American culture and in most cultures around the globe. Such a wide range of abuse can have deadly consequences. According to the state Attorney General's office, 29 percent of the homicides committed between 1984 and 1994 were rooted in domestic violence, compared with 15 percent nationwide. With such data revealing the serious magnitude of Hawai'i's domestic violence problems, the state's voters might expect the issue to be a high priority with state and county legislative bodies. But not much has been done—few bills are passed and little money is appropriated, especially in an increasingly tight local economy.

Would things be different if more women were in power? Consider the charges of sexual harassment against Senator Daniel Inouye during his 1992 reelection campaign, made by Inouye's election opponent, Republican state Senator Rick Reed. Reed secretly recorded conversations with Inouye's

Honolulu hairdresser, who, Reed claims, had engaged in sexual relations with Inouye against her will. The woman did not disavow Reed's remarks, but neither would she press charges against Senator Inouye, who won reelection—but by a smaller margin than he was accustomed to. While not passing judgment on Inouye, Martha Ross did say that the alleged incident is very common, particularly the reluctance of the alleged victim to speak out. "Sexual assault is the most under-reported crime in Hawai'i," she said, citing a state Attorney General's report that indicated that only about two percent of the nearly 10,000 women who had been sexually assaulted in 1993 actually reported such incidences. "I have no idea whether he [Inouye] is innocent or guilty of these charges," said scholar Cindy Kobayashi (Mackey) in the *Star-Bulletin*. "But what is significant to point out here is that because there was no real investigation into the matter, no one will ever know. All we have are the stories of a brave nisei soldier who has become the most powerful man in Hawaii."

Working Women

DBEDT reported that in 1990, 77.3 percent of all males were in the labor force, as were 63.3 percent of all females. Of adult women in the labor force, over half had children under six years of age. With nearly two-thirds of women in Hawai'i working, the state has the highest percentage of working women in the nation, 6 percent above the national average. Paid employment outside the home seems not to offer Hawai'i's women the political empowerment that money can bring, however. Women are more likely to offer volunteer (unpaid) services, rather than cash, to campaigns. They don't link their contributions to a quid pro quo. Because their services are unpaid, candidates tend not to recognize their financial value. Even the most successful, highest-paid women do not have the political clout that their male professional counterparts have. But then, there are so few. Of the top 30 highest-paid executives in Hawai'i, most are male.

Women and men do not do the same work in Hawai'i. Women heavily outnumber men in clerical and administrative support positions and also in service occupations. Men heavily outnumber women in precision production, craft and repair work, machine operation, assembly and inspection, transportation and material moving, farming, forestry and fishing. There is rough parity between the sexes in managerial positions, technical support, sales, and professional specialties such as medicine and dentistry. In a sense, men dominate "blue-collar" positions, while there is a sharing of white-collar work between men and women. The number of women in business as compared to men is more striking. Male-owned businesses outnumber female-owned businesses by 2 to 1.

Women also make less money than men, often even in the same positions. Labor scholar Michael F. Miller reports that the roots of sex-based wage discrimination in Hawai'i date back to the segregation of work or division of labor well before the monarchy period, but so, too, do efforts to lessen that discrimination. In 1852, penalties for breaking the "appropriate business of females"—that is, when a woman performed what was traditionally a man's work—were dropped.

In the early part of this century, women dominated the fields of nursing, teaching, dressmaking and other "female" jobs, a segregated pattern that soon included librarians, stenographers and social, hospital and cafeteria workers. The Honolulu Typographical Union, organized in 1884, is believed to be the first labor union in the islands, though some argue that the first was actually the National Teachers Association, which was formed in 1882, and later became the Territorial Teachers Association and the Oahu Teachers Association. A Honolulu Nurses Association was formed in 1917. The American Federation of Labor attempted to organize a teachers' local in 1919, but it was not much more than a paper organization.

Teachers' associations on O'ahu, Hawai'i and Maui eventually came together to form the Hawaii Education

Association (HEA) in 1921, electing a woman as the organization's first president. The HEA had chapters on all major Hawaiian islands by the 1960s, and was later reorganized into the Hawaii State Teachers Association (HSTA). "It has been through the participation of women that the unions are now addressing such problems as job segregation and sex-based wage discrimination," writes Michael Miller. The union with the largest number and largest percentage of women (60 percent) is the Hawaii Government Employees Association (HGEA), which came to prominence in recent decades and flexed its muscle during a 1994 strike (the parent union of the HGEA is the American Federation of State, County and Municipal Employees, or AFSCME, which is also the parent union of the United Public Workers, or UPW, which includes hospital workers and nurses). Jackie Ferguson-Miyamoto became the first woman to be elected HGEA president in 1997, although Russell Okata has wielded more influence as HGEA's chief negotiator.

Women have not organized in all work areas. Scholar Joyce Chinen notes that in Hawai'i's sizable garment industry, women have faced major obstacles to organization due to differences in age, generation and ethnic characteristics. The International Garment Workers Union, the Amalgamated Clothing and Textile Workers Union and Hawaii's International Longshoremen's and Warehousemen's Union (ILWU) have made minimal efforts to help organize women workers in the local industry (the latter union's international headquarters in San Francisco changed the ILWU's name to International Longshore and Warehouse Union in May 1997). Chinen believes it is crucial for these women to organize, for they are being "occupationally ghettoized" through a pattern of ethnic succession (that is, mostly Japanese-American women worked the garment industry following World War II, while mostly Filipino-American women have worked there in recent years). "In much the same way that the ILWU emphasized industrial unionism, and 'an injury to one is an injury to all' in the 1930s through the 1950s, they need to educate women workers that they are all 'sisters under the skin,'" Chinen says.

Scholar Marian H. Roffman has complained that, though Hawai'i has a larger percentage of working women than any other state, they are underpaid, concentrated in low-income jobs and discriminated against on the basis of sex. Women are also not well represented at leadership levels in unions, a fact explained by Hawai'i's history and ethnic population. The plantations were initially worked exclusively by men. Only later were women brought in and even then, only in numbers considerably smaller than the male population. According to Joyce Chapman Lebra in *Women's Voices in Hawaii*, men outnumbered women by 10 to 1 on the plantations. Workers from Japan and the Philippines were encouraged to obtain brides from home.

In 1923, a territorial attorney general declared that women should be taxed for independent income, just as men were. In 1933, the territorial governor established that rates of pay for positions in the government be fixed so that there would be "equal pay for equal work," an understandable change, given that women at this time made up 54 percent of the entire work force, including 83 percent of all teaching positions. In 1959, a law was passed providing for equal pay for equal work regardless of sex, religion or race. However, since statehood, little has been accomplished to address pay inequalities between men and women, wrote Miller. The HGEA achieved some success for public sector secretaries and nurses in the late 1970s and early 1980s, according to Miller, but occupational segregation remains the norm.

A report prepared by the state auditor in 1995 stated that female blue-collar and nonprofessional government workers earn an average of $350 a month less than their male counterparts. This pattern surfaces in food service, nursing, paramedical assistant and occupational therapy assistant occupations, the study reported. A survey by Community Resources Inc. reveals that, though women do earn less than men, the salaries of younger women are closer to men's salaries: in the 45-to-64 age bracket, females earn only 61 percent of males' salaries ($23,477 compared to $38,707); for the 35-to-44 age bracket, women earn 70 percent ($23,029 compared to $33,120); for the 25-to-34 age bracket, however, women earn 82 percent of a man's salary ($19,855 compared to $24,215). The survey takers concluded that gender, and not ethnicity, is a critical determinant in who will be successful in the workplace. "It appears that the economic value of a four-year college degree may be less than the economic value of simply having been born a male," the survey authors reported.

Certain fields have been more accommodating to women. According to writer John Luter, women generally have found more jobs as reporters on newspapers and magazines in Hawai'i than in most other states. A few have also served as magazine publishers and editors in past decades. As of the late-1990s, the publisher of the *Honolulu Weekly* is female, as have been most managing editors, while a woman is the editorial page editor of *The Honolulu Star-Bulletin* (in 1957, Elizabeth Farrington became president of the *Star-Bulletin* and KGMB Broadcasting upon the death of her husband, Joseph). Women have also been editors of *The Hilo Tribune-Herald, West Hawaii Today* and *The Maui News*, among other publications. The magazine *Hawaii Business* had until recently a female president, general manager and editors. *Island Business, Aloha* and *Honolulu* magazines have also had women on their editorial staffs. There are also female television news anchors, though they are invariably paired with males. Female news producers, directors and station managers are less common, however.

Hawai'i has its own Comprehensive Equal Pay Act to complement federal statutes. Unfortunately, says Coralie Chun Matayoshi, these laws have not always worked. "Part of the problem is that most discrimination is subtle and difficult to prove," she explains. "Unless a woman is fired, there is little incentive to endure the emotional and financial cost often needed to file a grievance."

Matayoshi notes that even though women have entered the work force in great numbers, many still view their primary role to be homemaker. "Women themselves often feel guilty about pursuing a demanding career that prevents them from being a 'good' mother or wife," she says. "And even the most liberal man would probably ask his wife to cut back on her career before hurting his own if two demanding careers proved detrimental to their family life." This problem is compounded by the necessity of two incomes per family in Hawai'i. "The already high and still rising cost of living here requires women at all economic levels to serve as either sole breadwinners or equal partners in bringing home the bacon. At the same time, society continues to demand that women bear most, it not all, of the burden of family care giving." Matayoshi does point to hopeful signs that things are changing, noting that medical, law, business and other schools are turning out women doctors, lawyers, masters of business administration and other professionals at an ever higher rate. "These young, educated women are working side by side with male colleagues generally more open to gender equality than their fathers were." Matayoshi notes that Hawai'i, in addition to being the first state to recognize women's reproductive rights, also has among the most liberal maternity-leave policies. Female employees disabled due to pregnancy, childbirth or related medical conditions are permitted to take a leave of absence for a reasonable amount of time.

Matayoshi also reports that the percentage of women working outside the home has tripled since 1950. Today almost half of Hawai'i's work force is female. Still, women are paid on the average 65 cents for every dollar a man earns. "Overrepresented in lower-paying jobs, women earn consistently less than men across virtually all job categories," Matayoshi says. "Studies have shown that differences in education, work experience and other objective factors account only partly for the wage gap." The wage gap is noteworthy in two professions where one might expect to find little discrimination: the law and higher education. Even when factors such as age, years in practice and position are constant, women earn only about 58 percent of the salaries of male attorneys. Additionally, women are less likely to be partners or supervisors and, while women are 20 percent of active lawyers in Hawai'i, none has taken a position on the federal bench in Hawai'i and only one has served on the state Supreme Court in the past 30 years. At the University of Hawai'i, until a recent equity adjustment, female faculty earned on average nearly $2,000 less annually than their male counterparts.

In the business world, Matayoshi reports, women hold only 9.1 percent of corporate directorships for the top 50 Hawai'i companies, though this percentage has been climbing. Unfortunately, the percentage of women CEOs and board chairs has actually slipped in the past decade. "The fact that the highest echelons of business in Hawaii are dominated by older males may keep women from rising to their full potential," Matayoshi says. "It's called a glass ceiling."

A Progressive History

Although Hawaiian women never shared equal status with men, Hawaiian women did enjoy a high degree of political power before white missionaries and merchants arrived in the nineteenth century. It was King Kamehameha I's favorite wife, Ka'ahumanu, who, after the monarch's death in 1819, convinced the new king, Liholiho, to break the *kapu* (taboo) tradition of not eating with female chiefs. Ka'ahumanu had previously broken *kapu* against eating pork and shark's meat, and she slept with other chiefs despite the fact that King Kamehameha had put a *kapu* on her body.

Gavan Daws notes in *Shoal of Time* that Ka'ahumanu had concluded that she need not fear retribution from the gods, but "only penalties exacted by male chiefs on behalf of the gods." When Kamehameha's son, Liholiho, assumed the throne, Ka'ahumanu created an office for herself in which she shared power with the king, effectively serving as Hawai'i's first queen from 1819 to 1832. In addition to convincing Liholiho to abolish the eating *kapu*, Ka'ahumanu succeeding in abolishing idolatry, and in 1824 on Maui established the first penal code for the Hawaiian Islands prohibiting murder, theft, fighting, and work as well as play on the Sabbath. She also established schools with compulsory attendance for adults and children. In 1825, Ka'ahumanu prohibited the traffic in and use of intoxicating liquors and made a general law against bigamy and desertion.

There were other notable Hawaiian women of this period. In 1840, a female chief named Kekauluohi served on the Hawaiian Supreme Court. Others served as governors and judges on various islands. High female chiefs wore feathered capes and helmets on the battlefield, shared equal property rights with men and served as Hawai'i's genealogists. Queen Emma founded Honolulu's Queen's Hospital, Bernice Pauahi Bishop founded the Kamehameha Schools, and Queen Kapi'olani established what would later be called the Kapiolani Medical Center for Women and Children, also in Honolulu. Emma Metcalf Beckley Nakuina was the first woman judge to serve the territory, noted Anne Russell. The Dowager Queen Emma challenged David Kalākaua for the throne when King Lunalilo died in 1874 after a short reign, but lost. A majority of the Hawaiians favored Emma, as did a band of Englishmen in the islands. The pro-U.S. faction opposed her, though, because of her preference for England over America. Kalākaua was thus the lesser of two evils for pro-U.S. forces. He won the battle for the throne, going on to rule for 16 years.

Kalākaua died in 1891 and was succeeded by his sister, Queen Lili'uokalani, Hawai'i's last monarch. Lili'uokalani was a "determined woman with definite ideas," according to author Edward Joesting. She had been critical of her brother's rule because he had given up royal rights to the white aristocracy without a fight. She insisted on naming her own cabinet, and the islands' Supreme Court upheld her wish. Hawai'i would not get a chance to see what kind of rule Lili'uokalani might have developed, for she was deposed by white merchants with U.S. support in 1893. The monarchy was abolished, and the nation of Hawai'i briefly became a republic. Soon it would become a territory of the United States under the Organic Act, an act of Congress that set up the government under which Hawai'i would be ruled for almost sixty years (the U.S. would formally apologize for that annexation a century later). Sanford B. Dole was appointed the first governor—he was already head of the Republic of Hawai'i, having been a key player in Lili'uokalani's overthrow—and governors and secretaries of the territory were subsequently appointed by the U.S. president, who also named all judges of higher courts. Citizens with Hawaiian blood would for many years dictate the choice of who sat in the territorial Legislature, for Hawaiians formed a majority of the electorate. Despite preferential treatment for Hawaiians, though, Hawaiian women would remain largely in the shadows for many decades.

Scholar Patricia Grimshaw notes that soon after their arrival in Hawai'i in 1820, and for the next three decades, New England missionary women embarked on a plan to educate Hawaiian girls and women about Western feminine values. The experience proved frustrating and sometimes tragic for both groups. The issue of sexuality particularly caused friction, for Hawaiian women had a far different view of sexual relations than the pious white women. White women also promoted the traditional American work and family roles of men and women. The Hawaiian women had difficulty adopting submissive behavior to men and family as a feature of feminine behavior and personality. "The notion of women's moral leadership in the marriage offered...a countervailing source of power to that given the man by right," Grimshaw notes. Hawaiian women, conversely, believed in a larger view of kinship that extended well beyond the nuclear family. "Their roles as sisters, daughters, nieces took precedence over the marriage bond as representing the reference point for status," she explains.

Grimshaw also adds that the positive contributions of the white missionary women are often overlooked by historians. These women taught many Hawaiians the necessary skills—especially reading and writing—to navigate Western society. White women were also instrumental in the establishment of the public school system.

The League of Women Voters of Hawaii was formed in 1922 by white women who worked on a variety of issues, including jury duty for women, rights for women in making wills and contracts, guardianship of children in case of death or divorce, health programs in the schools and joint property rights for married couples. Eventually they became interested in governmental affairs concerning women and children. A 1930 study showed that a few white women served as federal judges, territorial and city executives, and on territorial and city boards. By 1950, five women—four of them white, one Hawaiian—were members of the convention proposing statehood. Elizabeth Farrington succeeded her husband, Joseph, as territorial delegate to Congress after his death in 1954. Elsie Wilcox of Kaua'i was elected in 1932 as the first woman to serve in the territorial Senate. Several other women—most of them white—were interested in issues such as health, education and "women's activities." Marsha Rose Joyner noted in an *Advertiser* story that only white women or part-Hawaiian women with one parent on the "Big Five Circuit" could be a member of the inside political club. She cited Wilcox, Farrington, Sarah Todd Cunningham, Flora Hayes, Thelma Moore Akana and Bina Mossman as party "standard bearers" in the 1930s and 1940s. She also noted that Kaua'i Democrat Rosalie Keliinoi was the first woman elected to the Territory of Hawai'i Legislature, in 1925. Mary George became the first woman elected to the Honolulu City Council in 1968, and she later became a state Senator (George was hailed by Republicans and Democrats alike upon her retirement as the "conscience of the Senate"). Other white women have served as judges, beginning with Carrie Buck in 1925, the first woman assistant

U.S. attorney in Hawai'i, and later the first woman circuit court judge. But neither Polynesian nor white women have succeeded to high office since statehood except in rare instances, and even then usually only for a short time.

Haunani-Kay Trask writes in *From a Native Daughter* that the contemporary feminist movement in Hawai'i has failed native women, for it has been too concerned with "women issues" such as reproductive rights and employment. Trask says feminists—particularly white feminists—should instead help Hawaiian women with efforts to throw off colonialism. "In Hawaii, as in so many parts of the island Pacific, haole feminists have steadfastly refused to support our efforts to regain our lands, to protect our civil rights, and to achieve self-government," she says. Trask also believes that Hawaiian women have been in the front lines in the sovereignty movement, while Hawaiian men have followed a more established path because native men are rewarded for "collaboration" with the white and Asian power elite, while women who seek political power can only serve as adjuncts to men. "Our Native men have something to sell out for, our women do not," says Trask. Scholar Noenoe K. Silva has written that Hawaiian women in particular actively resisted U.S. annexation. Though Trask is correct in recognizing the instrumental role of Hawaiian women in the sovereignty movement—her sister, Mililani Trask, has headed the largest and most widely recognized sovereignty group, Ka Lāhui—it appears that Hawaiian men are increasingly asserting their leadership. Hayden Burgess (also known as Poka Laenui), Kekuni Blaisdell and Dennis "Bumpy" Kanahele, for example, have all emerged as outspoken critics of the American "occupation" of the islands, and each heads his own sovereignty group. Clayton Hee took an aggressive stand during his many years as chair of the Office of Hawaiian Affairs, although his leadership was challenged in 1997 by five female trustees, including the woman who replaced Hee as chair, Adelaide "Frenchy" De Soto.

AJA Women

While Hawaiian and white women have—with some exception—been less active active in state electoral politics, Japanese-American women have stepped to the fore. AJA women have been major candidates for governor, lieutenant governor and county mayors, and they are generally more active in public affairs than women of other ethnic groups. Thus, there is much more written about them than other Asians.

The first generation of Japanese women who immigrated to Hawai'i came as wives, mothers, sisters, housekeepers, cooks and laundresses. "As products of a tightly organized society where men ruled over women and where knowing one's place was more important than one's personal feelings, these issei women have been viewed by historians as being more restricted and bound by traditional Japanese culture and by the oppressive economic and social conditions of plantation life in Hawaii than issei men," according to scholar Gail Y. Miyasaki. "Their daughters, the nisei, inherited much of this view of Japanese women, even if they were American-born. Nisei women, for the most part, have not shared in the spectacular rise of the Japanese in Hawai'i after World War II. Instead, many of them have gained recognition as the wives of prominent nisei politicians, labor unionists, businessmen or professionals who participated in that rise."

Japanese-American women are often stereotypically portrayed. In the 1995 film, *Picture Bride*, a Japanese bride is featured accepting—after much soul-searching—her lot in life wedded to a much older Japanese plantation worker. That depiction of *issei* women as passive, dutiful and subservient is in sharp contrast to Laurie M. Mengel's research into *issei* women, who frequently filed for divorce from their husbands, citing drunkenness, cruelty and desertion.

Some Japanese women came to Hawai'i for other reasons. "Many of the earliest Chinese and Japanese women in America were prostitutes who had been lured, kidnapped, or sold into a trade which reaped rich rewards for Asian importers and brothel owners as well as for American officials, police, and landlords," note Elaine H. Kim and Janice Otani in *With Silk Wings*.

Many *nisei* women in Hawai'i became school teachers, secretaries and clerks, and qualified for the civil service, which, while not as exciting as the jobs held by their *nisei* brothers, advanced them into occupations not previously held by Asian women. Some also became involved in labor unions. Miyasaki notes that members of the Women's Auxiliary of the ILWU joined protests by striking longshoremen on the Hilo docks in 1938, where many people, including women, were injured when authorities intervened. Still, a great many women had few options other than service-industry jobs or domestic service. Evelyn Nakano Glenn, writing about similar experiences for Japanese women on the mainland during this time, terms the narrow field of opportunity an "occupational ghetto which trapped successive generations of women.... Japanese women were denied the resources and connections needed to move into other fields."

The Japanese concept of *ie*, central to an understanding of Japanese family and society, holds that males take precedence over females, older people over younger, and those born within the household over those born outside it. Authority, work responsibilities and privileges are assigned according to these criteria. Scholar Dennis M. Ogawa explains in *Kodomo no tame ni* that this patriarchy has gradually waned and been replaced with a strong matriarchal or bifocal family structure. Among third-generation Japanese descendants, or *sansei*, only one-tenth believe that the patriarch still rules the family. Ogawa also points out that first- and second-generation Japanese Americans often refer to the third generation as "spoiled." Ogawa says that from the *sansei* on, Japanese-American women acculturate much faster than males. "Men are much more traditional, while women are much more equal rights-minded," he says. "Men may say they are, but they really are not."

Scholars Terence A. Rogers and Satoru Izutsu explain that sex roles in traditional Japanese culture were strongly separated, but that the authority of women was far greater than has been generally understood. "In modern AJA families women have made the same kind of advances in status as they have in the rest of the United States, but probably to a lesser degree," they observed. "In any event, these advances have coincided with an erosion of the traditional authority of the males." In public, women will defer to men; but in the home, they control family finances, child rearing and other major decision-making. However, traditional expectations and emphasis on career opportunities for sons are the obstacles to women's entering learned professions. Traditional patterns of loyalty, reticence and group conformity add to the difficulties Japanese women have in breaking out of their positions. "Today, in a family with a progressive daughter, the tensions and resentment can be considerable if she questions her subjugated position, or if she demands her rightful share of the family's interest and support for her ambitions," according to Rogers and Izutsu.

Evelyn Nakano Glenn examined first- and second-generation Japanese-American women, as well as Japanese women who married American soldiers during the Occupation and then moved to the United States. It was in part a personal journey. "As a young girl I resented the whole notion of female subordination and the socialization it entailed," she writes in *Issei, Nisei, War Bride.* "I respected my mother, grandmothers and aunts for their selflessness and hard work. I appreciated their critical contribution to the family and the economy.... But, I vowed, I would not be like them. They were uncomplaining martyrs, catering to their husbands' demands and sacrificing endlessly for their children.... I viewed them as victims, and therefore as weak." Her interviews with eight San Francisco Bay Area AJA women changed her preconceptions. Glenn learned that these women were quite varied in personality and character. Triply oppressed in society—as women, as Asians and as menial laborers—they were not always passive sufferers. "It became evident that static models of class, race, and sex that would treat Japanese women simply as objects of history were inadequate and misleading." Glenn came to view labor exploitation and control as central to the oppression of Japanese-American women. "Racial-ethnic status and occupational position became more or less synonymous badges of inferiority," she wrote.

As scholar Joyce Chapman Lebra pointed out, immigrant women were not feminists; indeed, feminism as a movement had yet to appear when most groups immigrated to these shores. "For the women who settled in Hawaii, the chief concern was survival," she says. But in their struggle to feed and clothe their large families, they did so without complaint, sacrificing their own interests for the greater good. It is only in historical perspective that we see these women as oppressed.

Trailblazers

In spite of cultural constraints, several Japanese-American women have succeeded in Hawai'i politics. One is Maui native Patsy Takemoto Mink. In 1956 she became the first Asian-American woman to run for the Hawai'i Legislature, and six years later she was the first woman to be elected to the U.S. Congress from the state of Hawai'i (and the first woman of color nationally). Mink occupied the same seat for decades, though she left Congress for a number of years to pursue other offices. Scholar Anne Russell says that Mink's political success is remarkable, especially in light of traditional behavior of Asian women. "Japanese-American women in Hawaii showed high patterns of deference," Russell writes in "Patsy Takemoto Mink: Political Woman." "Their upbringing had roots in traditional Japanese culture, which emphasized female beauty and ornamentation along with patience, humility and non-aggression. Japanese girls did not press their opinions forward in the presence of boys, for overly talkative or intelligent types were not considered feminine.

Women were considered inferior from birth, to be subjugated and controlled by men."

Of the few women who were in politics up to the 1950s, almost all were white or Hawaiian and closely tied with established male business interests. Mink was the first to break this tradition, but her career has not been without difficulty. In 1959, after statehood, Hawai'i was entitled to one seat in the U.S. House of Representatives and two Senate seats. Believing Daniel Inouye would run for the Senate, Mink began to campaign for the House. At Jack Burns's urging, Inouye switched to the House race and defeated fellow Democrat and Japanese-American Mink. Mink ran successfully for the House in 1963, when Inouye moved on to the Senate. She still coveted higher office and had wanted to run against incumbent Hiram Fong in the 1970 Senate race but was dissuaded by family and friends. She deferred—to her regret, Russell reports—but challenged Japanese-American Democrat and fellow U.S. Representative Spark Matsunaga in 1976 to fill the Senate seat vacated when Fong retired. Matsunaga won that race handily. Russell's biography of Mink ends in the late 1970s. Since then, Mink has run unsuccessfully for mayor of Honolulu and for governor but successfully for a seat on the Honolulu City Council. She was also a candidate in Oregon's 1972 Democratic presidential primary. Mink returned to Congress in 1990.

Russell notes that Mink was encouraged by her parents from a young age to do as she wished. "They did not push her into depending on a boyfriend for her happiness or into molding her personality so that she would be pleasing to a future husband," Russell explains. "The only expectation was that Patsy develop her own unique skills so that she would grow into a competent, responsible, independent adult." Russell believes that this upbringing resulted in an adult who is "assertive, competitive, articulate, intellectually curious and high in self-esteem. These qualities are usual in men and unusual in women.... Women have learned through sex role stereotyping to limit themselves. Patsy Mink's horizons are unlimited insofar as she sees them. The fact that she is a woman does not enter into her goal-setting." This independence extended to her choosing of a husband who supported her ambitions. Russell calls Mink a "partial feminist," a woman who came of age before the women's movement of the late 1960s and early 1970s. By the time this movement was in full force, Mink was fighting for such issues as environmental protection, an end to the Vietnam War and early childhood education, though she later began to adopt a more feminist political perspective. Russell notes that Mink's reluctance to fully embrace the feminist movement has cost her support from some groups.

Not far behind Mink in entering Hawai'i politics was Republican Pat Saiki. After graduating from UH, Saiki first taught at Punahou School in Honolulu, then in Toledo, Ohio, where she accompanied her husband, Stanley, an obstetrician-gynecologist. She returned to Hawai'i and taught at Kaimukī Intermediate and Kalani High schools in Honolulu and won a seat as a delegate to the state's 1968 Constitutional Convention. She served as a state representative from 1968 to 1974, and then in the state Senate from 1974 to 1982. In 1983, she was named chair of the local Republican Party. Saiki ran unsuccessfully for lieutenant governor in 1982, was elected to the U.S. House of Representatives in 1986 and, after an unsuccessful bid for the U.S. Senate in 1990, was appointed by President George Bush in 1991 to head the Small Business Administration. She later taught for a semester at Harvard's John F. Kennedy School of Government and returned to Hawai'i in 1993 to run for governor.

A 30-minute television program titled "Hilo Girl" ran during Saiki's 1994 gubernatorial campaign. "I've been called a dragon lady," Saiki said, laughing, but she told the camera that she is also a mother, a wife, a family person. "My father always wanted a boy, so he called us each 'sonny boy.'" Her parents saved and sacrificed for their three daughters. "In those days girls were not considered worth investing in," she explained, but her father disagreed and instilled independence and confidence in his daughters. Saiki also talked about her late husband, who strongly supported her political ambition. "He was a partner...an advisor in politics...a secure man." All of their five children have also been involved in her campaigns.

Saiki also noted in the video that it was "tough" being one of the few women in the U.S. Congress, comparing the experience to a salmon swimming upstream. "My efforts to forward the cause of equal rights for women goes back to the days when I was the oldest of three girls," Saiki wrote the Hawaii Women's Political Caucus in 1994. "I sought to be judged in school, in sports and in social circles as an individual who could achieve in her own right." Saiki explained that in earlier years she was so busy bringing up her children and supporting her husband's career that she did not become politically active until after statehood. As a teacher at Kaimukī Intermediate, she helped form the first teachers' union in the state, the Teachers Chapter of the Hawaii Government Employee's Association. In 1969, Saiki was the first woman legislator to publicly endorse the right of women to choose to have an abortion. In 1972, she introduced in the state House an equal rights package of 25 bills, including the Equal Rights Amendment to the Hawai'i Constitution, which was passed and ratified. Saiki noted in campaign brochures that before she became involved in politics, a married woman could not have a credit card in her own name, nor a mortgage, nor maternity leave with job security.

Saiki has been disappointed that more women were not involved in politics, however. "It's unfortunate, but many women still believe there's something 'dirty' about politics that they aren't capable of fighting," she says. "That's wholly untrue. I can say as a woman that it's a decision-making process—that's all."

Despite her independent nature and push for women's rights, biographer Patsy Sumie Saiki (no relation) says, Pat

Saiki is somewhat traditional. "I don't ask my husband to do the dishes—not because it's right or wrong—but because I respect the tradition in which he was brought up," Pat Saiki said. She instructed her two sons, however, that they should make marriage an equal partnership. Bob Wernet, a former Honolulu journalist and advisor to local politicians—including Saiki—says that Saiki endorsed the ERA, is pro-choice on abortion and helped form a teachers' union because that was the sentiment of the state, even though such views were not typically Republican. Saiki is also pro-choice because her late husband was a gynecologist and performed abortions for women before the Supreme Court's 1973 ruling in *Roe vs. Wade.* Saiki herself puts it another way: "I'm socially liberal but fiscally conservative."

In many ways, Pat Saiki and Patsy Mink are similar. Both are "trailblazers," as Wernet puts it. "There may be a little bit of resentment among Hawai'i voters about Saiki, because her position required a good deal of outspokenness, independent thinking, bravado," he adds. "It is the opposite of 'quiet and effective,'" a phrase taken from one of former Governor George Ariyoshi's campaign themes. Noting that Mink has much the same personal qualities as Saiki yet has been in public office longer, Wernet attributes Mink's success to her being a Democrat. "Partisanship overrides everything. Had Pat Saiki been a Democrat, the 1994 election might have been a different story." But, even that might not have been enough. Japanese-American scholar Franklin Odo says of Saiki's unsuccessful 1994 gubernatorial campaign: "She talked too much. She revealed too much of herself. Many Japanese Americans were uncomfortable with her qualities and positions."

Aside from Pat Saiki and Patsy Mink—and Mazie Hirono, who also happens to be Hawai'i's first lieutenant governor born in a foreign country—successful Asian- American women politicians at higher levels have been rare. Among those, most have been of Japanese ancestry. Women of Filipino ancestry, by contrast, have largely been absent from politics. According to writer Helen R. Nagtalon-Miller, women of Filipino ancestry suffer from many misperceptions. The number of Filipino-American women educated and trained in the professions or white-collar occupations is low, thus giving credence to beliefs that Filipino women are not interested in or capable of pursuing higher education. This does not take into account that Filipino children born and educated in Hawai'i have had few role models to emulate, since the ratio of Filipino men to women was 10 to 1 on the plantations. Negative stereotypes have given rise to lowered expectations from teachers and employers. Still, several Filipino-American women have been elected to the state Legislature or appointed to prestigious state or county positions since the 1980s.

Writer Fred Soriano wrote that tensions that might be expected to develop when there is an imbalance between men and women in a given group have largely been mitigated by Filipinos through extended kinship. Filipino women have faced employment discrimination and have often been employed at the lower end of the wage scale, according to Robert N. Anderson and his co-authors in *Filipinos in Rural Hawaii.* The absence of women in Hawai'i has made it difficult to carry on the traditions of the Philippines; Filipino women in Hawai'i have considerably more freedom and control over the family than they would in their home country, and this is a threat to the stability of Filipino families. "As wives married to older men become more fully assimilated into Hawaii's society, they will be more likely to consider divorce as a means of improving their situations," the authors noted. In the job market, Filipino-American women are well represented, but again in lower-end jobs, reported Belinda A. Aquino. "The standard explanation for this imbalance is that Filipinos were the last immigrant group to arrive in Hawaii and they have not rooted themselves in the system yet," she stated (Aquino is the director of UH Mānoa's Center for Philippine Studies). Younger, newer, better-educated immigrants are challenging this position.

Writer Sarah Lee Yang says that in Hawai'i, women of Korean ancestry have sharply deviated from traditional Korean family systems, which include filial piety, regard for formal learning, and subservience to men. "In Hawaii, Korean wives took the major role in keeping the family intact, insisting on education of the young, and participating in activity in the larger community," she observes. Former state legislator Jackie Young explains that most Korean Americans are not as involved in U.S. politics because of the tumultuous political situation of South and North Korea, but that this is changing. Young also says that it is "not natural" for Asian women to run for office. "You have to have an exceptional husband," she says. Young quit school when she was 20 years old and reared four children. She returned to school at age 33, earning a B.A., M.A. and a Ph.D. studying at night while bringing up a family. Young later divorced and remarried, got involved in local politics and other community issues and was later elected the first Korean-American female state legislator in the United States. This is a matter of some pride to many in South Korea, Young notes. Her popularity there is surprising, given the patriarchal nature of Korea. "But Korean woman are very strong," Young notes. She adds that she and Jack Lewin discussed the possibility of running together as a team prior to the 1994 Democratic primary elections. Some Democratic insiders were relieved that Young lost that primary to Mazie Hirono, according to Young, not only because Hirono appealed to a larger ethnic group, but also because Young is considerably taller than Ben Cayetano, who would have been her running mate. "I was naive about the appearance factor," Young concedes. She praises Hirono's victory as a step toward political parity for women.

The Sex Factor

Hawai'i has not been terribly fertile ground for female politicians running for high office, though the state has shown progressive tendencies in other areas and a higher than national average for lesser offices. Why have women been largely unsuccessful running for the state's highest offices? Part of the reason may be that the state's cultures—Western, Asian and Pacific Island—all generally favor males, a prejudice that extends to other segments of society, including government.

Hubert S. Kimura suggests that women candidates can be more successful in Hawai'i by being fully aware of their "natural assets and liabilities." For example, women are perceived as more honest than men, and, because of cultural pressures, they are relatively immune from being verbally attacked by men in a campaign. "Criticisms from a man, no matter how well-founded, may backfire if the voters start feeling sorry for the women candidates under attack," Kimura says in *The Akamai Strategist*. Women who are mothers of small children can use family photographs to advantage in campaign brochures, hold signs with their children and give their children visibility in their campaign. Women can also "take advantage of uncontrolled television by proper use of make-up," Kimura suggests (male candidates today also receive facial cosmetic treatment for scripted or planned TV appearances). At the same time, Kimura explains, women have unique disadvantages in politics, such as concern for appearance, questions of femininity, inability to understand "men's" problems and marital status. "If the woman candidate is single, some voters may raise the question, 'why's she not married?'"

It is important to keep the "sex factor" in proper perspective, Kimura adds. "In most campaigns involving men and women candidates, the sex factor usually plays a minor role in the outcome of the election," he argues. "Only in extreme situations, a preoccupation with a candidate's sex becomes a widespread issue in a campaign." Still, a candidate's gender can be very important in terms of effectiveness in office. "Because a woman is more likely than a man to play the role of caregiver in the family, the woman legislator would understand the economic needs and health care concerns of the elderly," researcher Nanci Kreidman told the *Advertiser.* "Additionally, while many men and women officeholders are parents, the women have likely had more experiences related to child care and family support systems; this increases their concern as well as their desire to meet those needs for their constituents." Kreidman added that a woman will more likely consult a responsive and attentive leader, who will more likely be female than male.

Political writer Dan Boylan suggests that part of the reason why there are not as many female politicians in Hawai'i is the difficulty in attracting female candidates to run for higher office. "Pat Saiki and Patsy Mink are ambitious people, but if Saiki had wanted to, she could have stayed in Congress forever, as Mink pretty much has done," he says. "I think culture has something to do with the reason there aren't more women in office.... But it also has something to do with the nature of life in Hawai'i, which is that an awful lot of women have to work to help their families survive. This almost negates the chance for a childbearing woman from the outer islands to run, and that takes care of about one-third of all women [in Hawai'i], because they can't travel to Honolulu [where the state Legislature meets]."

The particularly difficult challenges women face in running for office in the islands are well symbolized by the career of Pat Saiki. An island-born, second-generation Japanese American and a descendant of plantation workers, Saiki's rise and success in local politics are notable, but, like Patsy Mink, she was not able to gain the top elective offices in three efforts. Her 1994 campaign for governor especially revealed the uphill battle women face in Hawai'i. Some say Saiki's heart was never in the governor's race, that the seat she truly coveted was the Senate seat she lost in a close, bruising 1990 race. Others argue that Saiki had been gone too long from local politics and was thus out of touch with local issues. Island Republicans asked her to run in 1994 because there were few other viable candidates and because of Saiki's ethnicity and gender. Ironically, it was these same characteristics which greatly contributed to her defeat by helping her Democratic opponents. Reporter Richard Borreca said, on the KHET "Dialogue—Elections '94 Forecast" program with Dan Boylan airing four days before the 1994 election, that another Japanese-American woman, Mazie Hirono, helped give Democract Ben Cayetano a broader base. Borreca pointed in particular to a television spot in which Hirono's grandmother addressed the camera in Japanese. Hirono denied that this spot was a flagrant appeal for Japanese-American votes, characterizing it instead as an effort to share with voters Hirono's personal qualities, particularly the importance of her family. "My family is what makes me *me*," she explained. "I felt I had to connect on this level."

Hirono also denied that her candidacy was directed by Democratic Party elders to counter Saiki's campaign for Japanese-American and female voters. "I decided on my own in 1992," she said about her candidacy. "I thought that Ben would run and I knew that he would need help." Cayetano's campaign manager, Charles Toguchi, concurred. "Mazie was independent and made the decision to run without any consultation from the so-called old boys," he said. "The same goes for Ben."

One clear factor in Cayetano's success was that the Democrats were able to present themselves as a united party. "There's no question that we are a ticket, the only one that is operating as a team," Hirono told local television. By contrast, the Republican ticket did not appear nearly so unified. Pat Saiki and her running mate, Fred Hemmings, rarely appeared together—in print, on television or in person—preferring to campaign independently. In the brief television spots where they did sit side by side, they looked somewhat uncomfortable with each other, perhaps because Hemmings had headed the Republican ticket only four years earlier. Saiki and Hemmings are also a generation apart in age, in contrast to Cayetano and Hirono, who are roughly of the same generation. Bob

Wernet credited Mazie Hirono with bringing a "cloak of tender respectability" to the lieutenant governor's race and, by extension, a warmth and softness to Ben Cayetano's campaign. Democratic activist Amefil Agbayani adds that Cayetano demonstrated during the campaign that he respected Hirono, acknowledged her competence and would treat her as an equal, and that voters—particular female voters—picked up on this.

Though Saiki had been the election front-runner for months, her campaign began to lose steam after her poll numbers steadily dropped once the primary election was over and the general election campaign began. Not coincidentally, this was when independent candidate Frank Fasi began a series of vicious attacks on Saiki, especially one in which the faces of Saiki and Cayetano were digitally "morphed" into the faces of Andy Anderson and George Ariyoshi, respectively, and then both into that of Big Island rancher Larry Mehau. The suggestion was that neither Saiki nor Cayetano—but especially Saiki—controlled their own campaigns. Bob Wernet believes that Fasi was the reason for Saiki's loss. "Frank Fasi was poisonous to this campaign," he says. "He can always count on about 25 percent of voters who want to see action before thought. He plays to those who love the spectator sports of politics. They want to see sparks fly. And that's what he did. He attacked Saiki's record in a way that was despicable. It was a blitzkrieg of Goebbels-style brainwashing of the electorate. It was a terrible disservice to the public and anathema to the electoral process. His campaign went way beyond negative." The Saiki camp was flooded with calls from supporters after one of Fasi's negative ads ran. Half the callers wanted Saiki to vigorously respond to Fasi, while the other half wanted Saiki to say nothing for fear that an aggressive Saiki would turn off voters.

Meanwhile, Cayetano benefited from Fasi's attacks on Saiki. With Hirono's help, playing up the softer side of Cayetano and playing down his toughness was a central element of his campaign strategy. This was not the same Cayetano who was born and reared in Honolulu. Cayetano was brought up by his father in a single-parent household (his parents divorced when he was five), an experience he said sensitized him to the difficulties faced by single parents, most of whom are women (the "latchkey" children theme would be used in many advertisements for both Cayetano and Mazie Hirono, who was reared by her mother and grandmother). Cayetano frequently mentioned his leadership in the after-school "A+" program in Hawai'i's public schools, an accomplishment that found inspiration in Cayetano's experience as a youth. He is pro-choice on abortion and supports public funding of abortions for those who qualify. In a campaign brochure and television commercial, Loretta Matsunaga, wife of state legislator Matt Matsunaga and daughter-in-law of the late U.S. Senator Spark Matsunaga, stated: "Ben gets it. He understands. You can be a female candidate and not get it."

Besides "getting" or understanding issues of importance to women, Cayetano appeared to have "got" another lesson: to tone down his personal image. His reputation during his early years and in the Legislature was that of a scrappy fighter. "I had my own bunch," Cayetano explained when talking about gang problems during the time he grew up in Kalihi. "We used to go around together, you know. We got into scraps here and there. Looking back, I thank my lucky stars that I didn't get into more serious trouble than fights and all that." Cayetano's father was a boxer, and Cayetano himself was an amateur boxer until his "brain told me not to take all that pain," but he still lists boxing as one of his favorite sports. "He is trying to soften his image somewhat, but he still has a wide streak of macho and a well-earned reputation for confrontation," observed reporter Kevin Dayton. "He said he has mellowed." Cayetano told Dayton that his parents separated in part because his mother used to dominate his father, but that his father was a "tough guy."

When Cayetano first ran for the state House in the early 1970s, he wore long hair in a "Prince Valiant"-type haircut.

His style was flamboyant, and for his court dates as a lawyer he wore then-fashionable platform shoes and a pin-striped suit. David Schutter, a former law partner, said that Cayetano was known as a tough negotiator and difficult to get along with. Schutter stated that he learned later that Cayetano was a "caring guy." In the 1994 campaign, Cayetano was able to submerge his rougher characteristics and play up his role as mature statesman. As *Honolulu Weekly* political writer Robert M. Rees noted, Cayetano stayed out of battles between Pat Saiki and Frank Fasi, who Rees said, "had punched themselves nearly into oblivion. The more Fasi and Saiki flailed, the better Cayetano looked."

Bob Wernet also believes that Fasi reserved his harshest criticism during the campaign for Saiki because Andy Anderson and the Republicans had chosen her over him. Some Republicans had wished that Saiki and Fasi would combine forces and run on the same ticket, but neither wanted to take the second spot. Saiki had already run for the lieutenant governor's seat, while Fasi had campaigned three times previously for governor. Besides, "Frank Fasi has a problem dealing with women in positions of authority," said Saiki. Dan Boylan, however, did not believe that Fasi ran out of revenge. "Fasi is by far the smartest, most imaginative, most innovative politician in Hawaii, and he got 90,000 votes because he has name recognition second only to God. The problem is that he is also the most arrogant son of a bitch the world has ever known."

James C.F. Wang notes that Frank Fasi has always been able to attract news, whether positive or negative. He is also a tough, macho politician. "Don't ever wait to be hit by the other guy," Wang quoted from a 1976 interview with Fasi conducted by the now-defunct *Hawaii Observer.* "You hit him first, and you don't get hurt." Some have speculated that Fasi holds a grudge against female politicians. "It's no secret that Fasi's ego was badly bruised when he was beaten by Eileen Anderson [in the 1980 Honolulu mayoral race]," observed local resident

Bob Kelsey. "At least when he lost his bids for governor it was at the hands of a man."

Fasi was upset that Republicans favored Saiki for governor in 1994. "Pat Saiki is a female Cec Heftel, and this election will prove that fact," Fasi stated, referring to the former Hawai'i Congressman who lost to John Waihee in the 1986 Democratic primary for governor. "We don't need Pat Saiki, she's out of the race," Fasi said of the League of Women Voters debate late in the campaign, though public opinion polls still showed the race to be close.

Writing about power in Hawai'i well before the election, the *Weekly*'s Robert M. Rees noted that Fasi was a fading political power: "His decline became apparent when he referred to his critics as 'ignorant housewives.'" Pat Saiki certainly would have disputed Fasi's irrelevance; her 1994 campaign worked hard to discredit him. A Saiki mailer asked, "Do you really trust Frank Fasi to be the next governor?" The mailer featured excerpts from newspaper reports on former Fasi-aide Kenneth Rappolt's recent federal corruption sentencing, and the Kukui Plaza development project scandal of the 1970s. "Frank Fasi has been waging a character assassination campaign" against Saiki, stated the mailer, a campaign which began when Saiki refused to step aside in favor of giving the Republican nomination to Fasi. The mailer included an excerpt from the *Honolulu Weekly* of August 31, 1994, that read: "Snarled Fasi to Republican Party Chairman Jared Jossem, 'I'm going to f— you. I'm going to f— Pat Saiki. I'm going to f— the Republican Party." The original *Weekly* article had printed the quotation verbatim, but the Saiki campaign chose to censor it mildly. The Saiki camp explained that it wanted to show voters Fasi's true nature but not push them in to voting against her for recirculating the entire remark.

Fasi had refused to challenge Pat Saiki in the Republican primary because, many believed, he could not defeat her. Too many members of the party had already aligned themselves with her campaign. (Fasi and his aides, such as Linda Wong, claimed that Fasi would have defeated Saiki in the primary if he had chosen to run, a claim only Fasi supporters believed.) Fasi seemed bent on delegitimizing Saiki's candidacy. "Basically, you're a decent person, except that you don't know what's going on," Fasi said of Saiki on local news after she complained about the notorious morphing ad, which alleged that others ran her campaign. "I run this campaign," replied Saiki angrily. "Nobody but nobody has veto power over anything except me." She decried Fasi's unethical behavior and defended the integrity of Larry Mehau and Andy Anderson, whom Fasi accused of running Saiki's campaign. "If Larry and Andy are honest, then you're looking at the pope of the Catholic church," countered Fasi. In one television spot that ran in the last week of the election, Fasi showed a line graph indicating that Saiki's support had dropped considerably over the preceding year and that she was far behind him, as he was about to surpass Ben Cayetano. These "statistics," however, contradicted Honolulu media polls (and the election's eventual outcome) and were intentional distortions on Fasi's part, just as the video segment of Fasi at the spot's close distorted the former mayor's actual features. Fasi was shown giving the "shaka" sign as he sat in a vehicle. The white-haired, weathered seventy-something Fasi of 1994 does not appear, but rather a considerably younger Fasi with black in his hair and few lines in his face.

In a 30-second radio spot that ran in August 1994, Frank Fasi charged that Pat Saiki had discriminated against women and non-white minorities in giving out loans while she headed the Small Business Administration, and, further, that Saiki was "corrupt, incompetent, dishonest." Truth-telling became a central issue, at least as far as Fasi was concerned. "Who's lying?" asked a full-page Fasi advertisement that ran in September and October in which statements from both Ben Cayetano and Saiki were compared with "the facts." One such "fact" was that Cayetano and Saiki both favored same-sex marriage, another clear inaccuracy on the part of the former mayor. Fasi would charge in October that Saiki had lied about her congressional record on authoring equal rights laws for women, to which Saiki replied that Fasi was lying. Fasi also charged that Saiki did not support the 1990 Family and Medical Leave Act, though Saiki stated that she had supported it in one of her campaign television commercials. President George Bush vetoed the Family Leave Act, but President Bill Clinton signed a revised form of the bill in 1993. Saiki, though no longer in Congress at that time, believed she had a right to share credit for the act.

Through all Fasi's spurious attacks, Saiki remained stuck in a damned-if-you-do, damned-if-you-don't position. A vigorous counter-attack might be viewed as unfeminine and inappropriate by voters. Decorous denials might be drowned out by the louder noise Fasi was making. Either way, she could lose votes to Fasi or Cayetano. The infamous morphing ad did not improve Fasi's poll numbers, for they remained essentially the same before and after the ad ran in mid to late-October. But Saiki was hurt by the ad—not because it suggested she was controlled by others, but because she responded angrily to it, a behavior perceived by some as unseemly for an Asian-American woman. Ironically, Ben Cayetano might have been helped by the same ad. As Amefil Agbayani has pointed out, the ad connected Cayetano to George Ariyoshi, thus improving Cayetano's image among Japanese Americans.

In an interview with reporter Mike Yuen, Andy Anderson observed that Pat Saiki at times appears stiffer and more "officious" than she is, and is criticized for occasionally reverting on the campaign trail to the style of her first full-time profession, school teacher. She sometimes sounds as if she were lecturing an audience rather than engaging it. She has also been called aloof. "When we started doing grass roots campaigning, with its hugging and kissing, she was uncomfortable doing that," Anderson explained, noting that she eventually grew more comfortable with the role. "All her life she's been competing for equality, for respect. She didn't want to lose what she had attained." Tom Coffman noted that Saiki appears wooden on television, which is in sharp contrast to Saiki in person. "She is fun-loving, vibrant, exuberant," he said. "But in her television ads, she looked stiff. She looked like she wasn't having any fun. And that hurt her campaign."

The League of Women Voters took issue with a television commercial run by Saiki near the 1994 general election that accused Cayetano of having a poor record on rape legislation while he was a state senator. "When a woman may drink too much, and then become the victim of rape...the penalty should not be as harsh," the spot quoted Cayetano as saying in a state Senate floor speech. Saiki's ad equated that remark with "blaming the victims." The League, however, said the ad distorted Cayetano's record and that he had not, as Saiki charged, fought to weaken penalties in rape cases. The 30-second ad, run late in the campaign, stated that as a legislator Cayetano had voted against courtroom privacy for rape victims, had called for a veto of a bill that would have made spousal rape a crime and voted against a measure that would have increased penalties for statutory rape of a child. "Cayetano's history is one of disregard for women," the spot said. "The 'shame' of this record is yours, Ben Cayetano." Saiki said that she chose to run the ad to counter Cayetano advertisements that he understands, or "gets," women's issues. Cayetano responded that Saiki's ad was a distortion of his legislative record, and that her campaign was desperate. "This is campaigning at its lowest," he charged. At a press conference, Cayetano said that Saiki was trying to inflame people's emotions, especially those of women. He demanded an apology from her, saying the ad was unethical and unconscionable and that it took his words out of context from the Senate journal. Mazie Hirono said the ad was a "tremendous disservice" to all women in the state.

But Saiki stood by it. Mary George, who co-chaired Saiki's campaign, said internal polls showed Saiki's female support diminishing after Ben Cayetano and Mazie Hirono captured the Democratic nomination, so the rape ad was run. "Ben knew he was vulnerable on this point—he's not exactly a champion of women's rights. It's not in his history, he's never introduced legislation to this effect—so he used women union members to successfully counter the ad." Hirono strongly defended her running mate and angrily denounced the ad, just as she would near the end of the campaign when a rumor was spread that Cayetano had impregnated a secretary on his campaign staff. The Hawaii State Commission on the Status of Women's director, Martha Ross, expressed disappointment that Cayetano never retracted his position on the legislation. "It was a very relevant issue," she said. "He should have said something, but the public didn't pick up on this."

To counter the Saiki ad, Hirono was featured in a full-page ad just before the election in which she accused Saiki of distorting Cayetano's record on women's issues. "Her campaign tactic of painting Ben Cayetano as anti-women, when the facts speak otherwise, insults the intelligence of Hawaii's women," the ad declared. Another Saiki spot echoed campaign literature in which Cayetano is quoted as saying, "There aren't any women's issues, as far as I'm concerned." The quotation is lifted from Cayetano's own 1994 campaign literature, but is taken out of context. In the original, Cayetano went on to say that "there are only people's issues."

Saiki's campaign literature emphasized her record on women's rights while at the same time showing pictures of her as beloved daughter, sister, niece, wife and mother—an appeal that highlighted not only her independence but her devotion to family. "From generation to generation, the values of our families have endured," stated one brochure with Saiki embracing her granddaughter while her elderly father smiles approvingly. That was not enough for some island commentators, however. *MidWeek* columnist Larry Price, in contemplating the style of the gubernatorial candidates, questioned the marital status of Pat Saiki, despite common knowledge of her husband, Stanley's, recent death. "Is she really a loner or does she have a significant other? Isn't anyone curious about whether she's married? If she is, why hasn't her husband put in a public appearance.... Is it possible Frank Fasi considers his spouse to be an asset, but Pat Saiki doesn't feel the same about hers?" Saiki wrote to Price to criticize his "mean-spirited" questioning of her husband. "My husband of 37 years was always my greatest supporter and confidant," Saiki wrote. "If you have never seen him during my 20 years of public service, it may be because you have never taken the trouble to cover politics as you should have." Saiki demanded an apology. Price refused and defended his column on the grounds that people "ask me all the time" about the personal lives of politicians.

Saiki said that a survey conducted by associates interested in running Saiki for governor in 1994 indicated that 95 percent of Hawai'i voters would not be opposed to having a female governor. In the waning days of the election, however, Saiki believed that an "old-style attitude" toward having a woman as governor developed, especially since Saiki's opponents were male. "In the final analysis, in a close election, you cannot dismiss that the gender card will be played by your opponents," she said. The "card" was intended for Japanese-American voters in particular, said Saiki, suggesting that Mazie Hirono was part of this card. "She was always three steps behind," said Saiki. Hirono publicly presented herself as the "second" to Cayetano. It was not overtly sexist or racial, but it was a strategic move. Saiki said she herself received advice to play to the tastes of particular voters, but she replied that it's not her style to be complacent and deferential. Saiki did not suggest that Hirono compromised herself, and in fact argued that Hirono is much like herself in that she was outspoken and an aggressive legislator. Hirono saw an opportunity—the lieutenant governorship—and took it. Saiki added that she feared Hirono, whom she credited for strong leadership on several important matters in the Legislature, would be "shut out" of the power process as lieutenant governor.

Saiki's campaign co-chair Mary George said that Hirono was a "tough cookie" but that she was "very soft all the way through [the 1994 campaign] from the TV ads and coverage, her pictorial image, her make-up and wardrobe, the colors she wore. She was a smart dresser, very chic, had an Oriental flare and kimono folds in her dresses and necklines. This contrasted with Pat, who wore tailored suits and pants." Saiki's fashion consultant recommend that she change her hairdo from a "bubble" to a sheared look that George and Saiki thought was too harsh. The consultant also recommended that Saiki wear round earrings and sharper necklines. For her part, Hirono denied that she received any coaching on her campaign appearance or that she tried to appeal to voters in this regard.

Mazie Hirono joined the Hawai'i Democratic Party in 1972 as a member of a group that supported George McGovern for president. Born in Japan, she moved with her mother and two brothers to Hawai'i at age eight. Her mother, a single parent, worked two jobs to support the family. They often changed residences, and Hirono attended five public schools. She graduated from Kaimukī High School and the University of Hawai'i, where she was awakened to politics by the Vietnam War. She later earned a law degree from Georgetown University. Hirono originally wanted to be a social worker, but changed her mind when she realized that there were "better ways" to change society. She stayed in the Legislature for 14 years and was viewed as one of the party dissidents, not afraid to take on difficult challenges. Hirono is married to an attorney. When she was in her early forties, the couple tried to have a child. After a miscarriage, Hirono decided to give up what she believed would be a difficult path to getting pregnant again. "I've made my peace with it," she says, choosing instead to grow closer to the children of relatives.

Hirono lost her position as chair of the House Committee on Consumer Protection and Commerce in 1984 when she supported state Representative Peter Apo in a House leadership struggle with then-Speaker Henry Peters. Hirono and others argued that there was a conflict of interest after Peters was named a trustee of the Bishop Estate. Hirono had a high success rate of passing housing, consumer protection and insurance reform bills. About Jackie Young's challenge to her candidacy for lieutenant governor, Hirono said, "We don't have enough women in leadership positions, so we should not be running against each other." However, Hirono also noted that it was an "interesting phenomenon" that women voters got to choose between two Democratic women for lieutenant governor. Hirono believed that the women's vote was a force that could be mobilized for the election.

Jackie Young, noting her long record of promoting women in politics, agreed that women running against each other was a "sign of strength." But Hirono had endorsements from nearly every major union, including the Hawaii Government Employees Association—a disappointment to Young, who was a longtime member of HGEA. Mike Yuen wrote that both Young's and Hirono's advisors made use of their candidate's physical attractiveness when promoting their respective images. Hirono handed out floral bookmarks during her coffee-hour meetings with supporters, observed graphic designer Roger Yu. He and graphic designer Carole Goodson thought that Hirono might have been trying to play off the "old boy network" theme and emphasize her femininity. Hirono is now part of the established Democratic network, and there is a strong possibility that she will be a future candidate for higher office. "The lieutenant governorship has been the only stepping stone to the governorship since Hawaii's Democrats established their monocracy in 1962," notes Dan Boylan. Hirono may well go on to higher office, but the mysterious power brokers so often alluded to in the 1994 campaign were never referred to as "the old boy and *girl* network."

Though Mazie Hirono arguably appealed to a larger ethnic group (Japanese Americans), her main primary opponent in

1994, Jackie Young, has had more ties to the women's movement. Young is also closely connected with the Korean-American community in Hawai'i. Their contest was a dilemma for Democrats, because both are well-liked. Young was first elected to the House in 1990 and was the first woman to serve as the state House Vice Speaker, in 1994. She is a former chair of the Hawaii Women's Political Caucus and a former first vice president of the National Women's Political Caucus. She also worked for the state Department of Education as a teacher and as a specialist dealing with students with disabilities. In 1990, Young said she was told that she was the wrong age, wrong gender and wrong ethnicity to win a House seat in the Lanikai-Waimānalo district. She won handily. Young is one of the few Korean-American politicians in Hawai'i. Her parents worked hard to send her and her brother to Punahou School; the Youngs entered the school because of an Asian quota. Young claims that her family was the first Asian family to buy a home in Honolulu's Mānoa Valley. Young was named by Governor Cayetano to direct the Office of Affirmative Action, an office later eliminated due to budget cuts.

Norma Wong, a Waihee administration official, was rumored to have been a possible candidate for the Democratic ticket in 1994, according to the *Honolulu Weekly*'s Derek Ferrar. Her candidacy was believed to have been supported by John Waihee himself, who was "floating a trial balloon" to test Cayetano's popularity, according to the *Weekly*. Larry Price argued that some have pointed out that Cayetano favored Honolulu City Council member Ann Kobayashi as his running mate, but she declined and ran for Honolulu mayor instead. Privately, Saiki supporters were relieved when Kobayashi lost the Honolulu mayoral race, for it was believed that one female in high office would be a threat to the election of another woman, namely, Saiki.

Once Hirono had won the primary, her campaign merged well with Cayetano's. The two—invariably referred to as "Ben and Mazie"—were presented as a comfortable package to the electorate, frequently appearing together in print and television advertisements, as well as at personal appearances. When their team was victorious on election day, the *Star-Bulletin* proclaimed—as if the winners were a romantic couple—"IT'S BEN AND MAZIE." Cayetano graciously credited Hirono as a major factor in their victory; she brought Japanese-American voters to the ticket, just as he brought Filipino-American voters. Cayetano also credited his wife, although the couple was separated during the campaign. Cayetano filed for divorce in May of 1996, citing irreconcilable differences (the couple had been married since he graduated from Farrington High School in the late 1950s). After the divorce, the governor married Republican small-business person Vicky Liu in May 1997.

Gay Marriage

The political campaigns of female office-seekers are not the only way that sex and gender issues play out in Hawai'i. Domestic violence, workplace issues, the family-values agenda of the religious right and same-sex marriage have all engaged the political energy and imagination of the state in recent years.

Same-sex marriage has been a topic of considerable interest in the islands and elsewhere since the Hawai'i Supreme Court ruled in 1993 that the law could not discriminate against such couples who wish to form a legal union. The Supreme Court sent the case back to the Circuit Court with the instruction that the state must demonstrate a strong rationale to deny same-sex marriage licenses. "The state can discriminate if it can show a compelling reason to do so," explained scholar Cori Lau. "Whether it has a compelling reason to prevent same-sex marriage must now be argued in a lower court, but most lawyers are predicting that the state will lose and that same-sex marriages will be allowed." The state under Governor John Waihee proposed a "domestic partnership" law which would limit the rights and responsibilities of same-sex couples. Dan Foley, a lawyer representing three same-sex couples in the Hawai'i case, felt that extending some but not all benefits to same-sex couples is still discriminatory. He believed the case could thus continue up to the U.S. Supreme Court. James Hochberg, a member of the legislatively- created Commission on Sexual Orientation and the Law, however, denies that same-sex marriage is a civil rights issue, akin to racial discrimination in employment, housing and public services. "It should be obvious to everyone that sexual orientation and issues of race and gender are not the same," he has written. "Race and gender are immutable characteristics, sexual orientation is not." He argued further that homosexuals are forcing the state to legitimize homosexual relationships, which Hochberg views as contrary to what is best for children, as well as a burden on social and health services. Fellow Commission member L. Kuumeaaloha Gomes countered: "This issue is about addressing fundamental human rights." The Legislature did pass a reciprocal benefits package, allowing any two adults who cannot marry each other to at least receive medical insurance rights, but *Honolulu* magazine reported in 1998 that the bill has been a "bust," as only a handful of couples applied for the benefits.

The issue of same-sex marriage has not been a popular one among Hawai'i citizens. An August 1994 *Advertiser,* Channel 2 News and SMS Research and Marketing Services Inc. poll concluded that 45 percent of voters would choose to vote for or against a candidate based on his or her position on same-sex marriage. More recent polls have indicated that opposition to same-sex marriage has increased to 70 percent. Despite the state's reputation for liberal-mindedness on social issues, Hawai'i citizens are frightened by gay marriage and organized opposition has capitalized on their fears. Prominent among those waging the battle against same-sex marriage are fundamentalist Christian groups and other conservative organizations.

Religion in Hawai'i is as varied as the people who live here, but the religious right of the mainland has had difficulties making local inroads. According to a *Weekly* article by Derek Ferrar, the religious right, led by such organizations as the Christian Coalition, which has a chapter in Hawai'i, believes it has an agenda that will eventually be adopted by island residents. That agenda is identified as "pro-family"— and against non-heterosexual unions. One important strategy of these activists is distributing "voter guides" to local churches, pamphlets that use question-and-answer formats to identify candidates whose views are closer to the Coalition's goals. Others in the religious right movement have seized on School Community Based Management (SCBM) as a way to exercise political influence. SCBMs are local school boards made up of parents, community representatives, administrators and students. They are not employed in most Hawai'i public schools, which are supervised by an elected statewide board. An American Civil Liberties Union (ACLU) staffer believes that SCBMs are a "Trojan Horse." Because it is relatively easy to get elected to a small-district SCBM board, religious conservatives can use such positions to curtail sex education and condom distribution. UH Mānoa professor and chair of the Green Party of O'ahu, Ira Rohter, has also warned of religious fanatics posing as "mainstream conservatives" with other hidden agendas.

The Rutherford Institute, which bills itself as an anti-ACLU organization, has worked to get the government to accommodate a variety of religious views, according to the *Weekly*'s Ferrar. Rutherford's director, James Hochberg, chairs the outspoken anti-gay organization Hawaii's Future Today. Rutherford also challenges legislation that prohibits employment discrimination against gays. Among the groups working for gay rights in Hawai'i are the ACLU and the local chapter of the Japanese American Citizens League, which has recognized that discrimination to some is discrimination toward all.

As a result of Pat Robertson's 1988 presidential campaign, some 7,000 new members, mostly conservative Christians, joined the local Republican Party and won leadership positions within the party, a development that prompted some elected Republican officials to change parties. One of those, O'ahu politician Ann Kobayashi, was told that she would not receive Republican endorsement because of her pro-choice position on abortion. Several other female Hawai'i Republicans, including Donna Ikeda, did the same. The movement in Hawai'i has not subsided, only retrenched, wrote Ferrar. The religious right has toned down its rhetoric against gays and abortion and instead focused on economic issues. Frank Fasi and Stan Koki were two candidates who embodied the spirit of the religious right in 1994. Koki, who ran for lieutenant governor in 1994 and 1998, was a player in Robertson's 1988 presidential campaign in Hawai'i and has been associated with religious-right activist groups, according to Ferrar. Fasi appeared on Robertson's television program. In 1994, he identified himself in radio and print ads as an anti-abortion Christian candidate. The *Advertiser*'s Greg Wiles noted that Koki downplayed his connections to conservative religious groups in 1994, as the religious right had not been very successful in recruiting members locally. Wiles also noted, however, that members of these groups are becoming more sophisticated in their techniques and are especially learning their place in the local political scene.

The 1994 Green Party gubernatorial candidate, Kioni Dudley, spent more than 15 years with a religious teaching order in Illinois, the Brothers of the Holy Cross, though he made little mention of it during his campaign. In the same election, Fred Hemmings, a self-proclaimed devout Christian, also downplayed his religious beliefs, possibly to distinguish himself from his primary opponent, Koki, and because he was sensitive to Hawai'i's celebrated tolerance for religious diversity. A 1996 survey found that over half of island residents were religiously unaffiliated, 34.4 percent followed a Judeo-Christian faith (of these, Roman Catholics comprised more than 213,000 followers; Mormon numbers ranged between 38,000 and

53,000, depending on the source, while Jewish numbers were below 16,000), 7.2 percent were Buddhists, and 7.2 percent followed another faith. One of the authors of the survey, however, argued that over four-fifths of Hawai'i's population believed in "some higher power" whether they were involved in an organized religion or not. "Cultural and religious values are very important to the people of Hawaii, by and large," said UH Mānoa religion Professor Ramdas Lamb.

The issue of same-sex marriage became central during the 1996 election. Several powerful state legislators lost their seats in part because of their stands on the issue, and the Senate president nearly lost his—even as the matter was being decided in the courts. However, another voter decision in 1996—to hold a constitutional convention in 1998—may lead to an amendment that would ban same-sex marriage rights; state courts ruled that "yes" votes for the convention did not exceed blank ballots, thus necessitating placing the question before voters in 1998. The same-sex amendment will reach voters another way, courtesy of the state Legislature, whose 1997 legislative session was dominated by same-sex discussion. Voters in 1998 will decide whether the Legislature should amend the Constitution to reserve marriage rights to heterosexual couples. The issue also arose during the 1996 battle for Hawai'i's 1st Congressional District seat: Neil Abercrombie—one of the most liberal politicians in the United States—endorsed traditional marriage between a man and a woman rather than support same-sex marriage.

Openly gay activists are beginning to run for office themselves. In the 1994 governor's race, Frank Fasi refused to debate one of his primary opponents, Best Party candidate Bill Woods, a former executive director of Honolulu's Gay Community Center and publisher of a monthly gay newsletter. Woods claimed that he was running against Fasi to "stop corruption" but he arguably was also running to promote discussion of gays' civil rights. Fasi, who wooed religious conservatives and anti-abortionists, once responded to a question asking whether he would appoint openly gay people to a governor's cabinet: "Absolutely not!" He said that if he had been governor in 1991, he would have vetoed a legislative bill that banned job discrimination on the basis of sexual orientation (Governor Waihee signed the bill). Fasi had proclaimed a "Gay and Lesbian Pride Week" while Honolulu Mayor in 1991.

Gender Politics

The *Star-Bulletin*'s Richard Borreca wrote prior to the 1994 election that the year was indeed momentous for women candidates because of the relatively large number of women who ran for office, but that the "women's vote" was less a phenomenon in Hawai'i than on the mainland. Quoting unnamed sources, Borreca suggested that gender is "less of a friction-causing issue" in the islands, that women were likely to respond to issues of interest to them, such as children's welfare, health care, domestic violence and education, but that female candidates were held to a higher standard than males.

This seems to be a factor in elections. Hawai'i's Legislature is, as it has always been, heavily male, though it has had high-profile female members, including in recent years Donna Ikeda, Barbara Marumoto, Annelle Amaral, Malama Solomon and Cynthia Thielen, among others. The state Board of Education, which has elective seats, also has several female members, one of whom chaired the Board in 1994. Besides Hirono, however, U.S. Representative Patsy Mink, who handily won reelection in 1994, is the only other woman who currently occupies a top elected position. Former Honolulu City Council chair Marilyn Bornhorst succeeded Richard Port as chair of the state's Democratic Party in 1996, but once again only a few female politicians were elected to office.

Although several powerful male state legislators lost in the 1996 general election (including Republican Michael Liu and Democrats Milton Holt and Jim Shon) and Republicans gained several seats, Democrats maintained their strong control of the state Legislature. A trans-sexual candidate, Tracy Ryan, lost a race for the state Senate to incumbent Carol Fukunaga. The total number of female legislators elected to office in 1996 was slightly lower than in 1994 due in part to high-profile losses for incumbents Donna Ikeda and Annelle Amaral. Lastly, Green Party candidate Keiko Bonk finished second to incumbent Hawai'i County Mayor Steve Yamashiro, a Democrat, but ahead of three other male candidates.

In a *MidWeek* column praising political underdogs, Dan Boylan encouraged voters to ("all things being equal") vote for a woman, as only one-fifth of state legislators in 1994 were females (as Boylan correctly predicted, that percentage would drop to less than one-tenth after the election). Ann Kobayashi was seen by many to benefit by being the only well-known female candidate for mayor among several well-known males; her third-place showing in a large field seems to support that contention. However, a poll conducted by the *Star-Bulletin* and Political/Media Research Inc. shortly before the mayoral election showed that the second-place finisher, Arnold Morgado, enjoyed a "wide margin of support" with women as well as voters of Japanese descent. In effect, Kobayashi and Morgado drew from many of the same voters.

It is not clear who the state's largest organization of women, the Hawaii Government Employees Association (HGEA), voted for in recent elections, though their leadership regularly endorses the Democratic ticket. Richard Borreca wrote that the candidates for governor in 1994 had difficulty addressing HGEA's spring labor strike, but that each candidate, especially Pat Saiki, should have embraced the strikers. "To many, the strike is not just about more money, it is about discrimination against women, because most members of the two bargaining units on strike are secretaries and office workers and most are women," he wrote. "If...I were picking sides for the political fight of my life, I would pick these women for my team." Over the past decade, the HGEA has seen its membership shift from being predominantly male and Japanese to mostly women and a growing number of whites, according to the union's executive director.

All candidates for governor in 1994 took strong positions against domestic violence, calling for more shelters, counseling and increased punishment for offenders, but domestic violence was not a major issue in the 1994 campaign. In an article accompanying the candidates' positions on domestic violence, Cori Lau stated that the next governor would have to do more than merely propose a budget and hand it to the Legislature. "He or she must play an active leadership role, lobbying, fighting for the money to help those citizens least able to help themselves," she said. "Hopefully the next governor will also propose longer-range, imaginative programs that focus on prevention, not retribution." Ben Cayetano has not. The Hawaii State Commission on the Status of Women, reflecting on data from a 1993 report on increased domestic violence in the islands, stated that solutions designed to fulfill the legislative mandate should include recommendations for ways in which violent behavior can be minimized or eliminated, statements that nonviolent behavior can be learned, and that healthy family relationships and individual self-esteem needed to be encouraged. These aims could be achieved through increased education, including more programs in public schools, direct action (either legal or legislative) and more research.

Mazie Hirono, though she has never claimed to have been the victim of domestic violence, stated shortly after the 1994 election that friends of hers had been victims, and her own mother suffered psychological abuse from her father, who was neglectful and drank and gambled. That behavior led to her mother's moving her and the Hirono children to Hawai'i from Japan. Hirono's grandparents helped to rear the children while Hirono's mother worked. Hirono calls her mother's decision to leave her husband in 1950s Japan "extraordinary. You were considered chattel." She has had no contact with her father since her mother left him. Hirono attributed her own success to a family that had many strong female role models. She also credited Betty Friedan's *The Feminine Mystique* with having made a big impression on her. As she told Robert M. Rees, "When I read the book in college, I realized I might have to take care of myself and not just get married and be taken care of."

Domestic violence is increasingly making headlines, confirming that it is found at all levels of local society. For example, State Representative Dwight Takamine of the Big Island served six months probation in 1997 for pushing his wife during a quarrel at their home. Blase Harris, Hawai'i's Libertarian Party chair, sees similarities between treating relationship problems and dealing with government problems. "Like abused spouses, voters keep going back to Democrats and Republicans and believe the same lies over and over again," he said. "They can't leave until they realize they can take care of themselves."

"THE PROMISE OF HAWAI'I"

HAWAI'I IS A unique and exemplary American state. Although it shares with the nation the unfortunate tendency to bring its prejudices about money, color and sex into the voting booth—as well as the board room, the schoolyard, the front page and practically every corner of island society—it also possesses tremendous potential to transcend these prejudices and become a true multicultural, democratic society. Hawai'i is the most geographically isolated society on the globe; yet, as it enters a new century, the world is quickly coming closer to Hawai'i. In only the last generation the islands have witnessed the implementation of satellite transmission and fiber-optic cables that—through telephone, fax, modem, television, radio and print—bring mainland U.S. and world events to Hawai'i's front door and bring Hawai'i to the world. These technologies and others will continue to bring many changes to the islands, including new modes of behavior that will likely influence traditional island customs. The raising of political consciousness among island groups is probable, as are expanded roles for women and gays. However, Hawai'i residents may also sympathize with initiatives of exclusiveness that have emerged elsewhere in recent years, such as anti-immigration legislation, English-only amendments, ends to affirmative action and gay rights denial.

Hawai'i is also aging, and generational differences will become more pronounced, especially as the pre-World War II generation passes. A Census Bureau report estimated that Hawai'i's elderly population—residents 65 years and older—will nearly double by 2020, with a dramatic rise in the number of people over 85 years of age. These estimates place Hawai'i among those states with the highest percentage of elderly.

The islands have seen changes in retail markets that have lowered consumer prices, while rents and housing costs have begun to level off and even drop. Though more and more residents are choosing to relocate to the mainland, even greater numbers are taking their place in the surf and sun. But, unless the state can modify its economy to be less reliant on tourism and military expenditures, the state and its people will forever be vulnerable to outside forces. "What I don't want to see is old plantations replaced by new plantations in hotels," Ben Cayetano said once. "They become new plantations only if we allow them to grow to a size where too many of our people are in it." That may already have happened. Almost half of all jobs expected to be created by the year 2005, according to *The Honolulu Star-Bulletin*, will be in the service industries.

It is difficult to imagine Hawai'i's people proposing to curb their islands' dependency on tourism, though this is what some sovereignty groups have proposed, as have some scholars, politicians and journalists. Many—including some state legislators—have proposed that gambling be legalized in order to aid the state's ailing economy. Hawai'i is one of only a few states that does not allow casino gambling or lotteries; some legislators have suggested that casinos operate on ships off shore. But this is reliance on the visitor industry.

Rather than sustaining its troubled political status quo, Hawai'i should instead look to new leaders and new ideas, ones that consider the needs of *all* island residents. It will be radical, and it will be difficult. But, the people of Hawai'i deserve the chance to fulfill its bright promise.

Empowering the Electorate

One thing that may help Hawai'i's future is the telecommunication explosion that has vastly improved the spread of knowledge. The 1994 election marked the first use of cyberspace in local elections. A state-developed service called Hawaii Inc. allowed Internet users direct communication with candidate platforms. Any candidate for any office could have personal and background information as well as platform or position papers presented on bulletin boards accessible via the Internet. Anyone who had a computer and modem or used a Hawaii FYI terminal in a public library could access this information. They could not only read information about participating candidates but also ask questions of the candidates. However, only a few people took advantage of the service.

Still, such services may become commonplace in the future and open the door to greater participation in island democracy. In 1996, Hawai'i's Democratic Party provided for Internet participation during its three-day state convention, with hook-up services donated by Oceanic Cable and Pacific Information Exchange Inc. At about the same time, U.S. Senator Daniel Inouye became the first member of Hawai'i's congressional delegation to post a World-Wide Web page in cyberspace. Inouye made the move after being swamped with pleas from constituents who wanted more information from him, the *Star-Bulletin* reported. Inouye's Web page includes up-to-date information on legislation that the senator is sponsoring, plus speeches he has given entered into the Congressional Record. Local newspapers and television stations have also begun to establish Web sites or home pages. There is even a "Nation of Hawaii Links" page that provides information on sovereignty, including differing views from such organizations as Ka Lāhui and the Office of Hawaiian Affairs. However, Hawai'i is still a long way from a computer and modem in every household, even if every voter wanted to use such tools as a political resource.

There have been other efforts to widen and diversify political participation in the islands. The 1994 elections, for example, were distinguished by "Price of Paradise 1994," or "POP '94" for short. POP '94 began as an outgrowth of Randall Roth's two *Price of Paradise* books which examined issues he and his contributors deemed critical to Hawai'i. POP '94 was a nonprofit, nonpartisan, civic-minded effort to generate questions for the top gubernatorial and mayoral candidates— questions not from experts and media, but representatives from ordinary citizens. Most of the candidates for these offices participated in POP '94 forums conducted with the help of *The Honolulu Advertiser* and television station KHON. POP '94 interviews aired throughout the campaign, and the *Advertiser* devoted considerable space to candidates' responses to POP '94 questions. Sensing a strategy that might sell more advertising space, the *Advertiser*'s competitor, the *Star-Bulletin*, initiated its own issues campaign, "Power '94," and enlisted the support of KHON's chief rival, KITV, but theirs was not a grass-roots initiative.

Most of POP '94's leaders were educated whites or Asians, and most were male. "We could have sought a better cross section of the community," wrote Herb Cornuelle in an executive summary mailed to POP '94 members and supporters. "More young people, fewer old people, fewer haoles, more people from rural Honolulu and the neighbor islands, more business types." But, as the *Advertiser*'s Jerry Burris noted, people who get involved in movements such as POP '94 are those who have the time and initiative—in other words, a *small* percentage of the island population. POP, however, represented far more diversity than the usual media representatives, and its membership was open to anyone. Community issue meetings were held not just in Honolulu, but in Windward and Leeward O'ahu and on neighbor islands.

Some questioned POP '94's ties with the media establishment. At least one critic, the *Honolulu Weekly*'s Robert M. Rees, saw POP '94 as little more than media self-promotion led by power elites. "One of the funny things that happened to POP '94 on the way to the forum was its co-opting by the establishment," he wrote, adding that the promising ideals that POP '94 held gave way to the dictates of the mass media, such as limiting the number of candidates that could be interviewed. But, POP '94 generated considerably *more* voter attention than previous elections had seen. More than 4,000 questions were submitted by *Advertiser* readers who filled out POP '94 coupons. These were winnowed down to 250 questions for the July POP '94 forum. After POP citizen panels interviewed candidates, KHON Channel 2 presented the answers, while TV station KIKU translated them into Japanese and Tagalog. 'Ōlelo public access television also presented the POP '94 program as well as its own forum, "Candidates in Focus."

POP '94 had its critics. Some pointed out that, after answering the POP '94 questions, candidates were rarely cross-examined. Not all candidates were interviewed, either. "Interviewing all 24 pre-primary candidates and effectively publicizing their responses wasn't feasible," explained Randy Roth. Though progressive and populist, POP '94 produced mixed results. "Television and radio stations plus newspapers were joined in a campaign to rigorously examine the state, ask the right questions of all the candidates and double-check the responses with the public," said the *Star-Bulletin*'s Richard Borreca of the 1994 campaign. "Of course, by the end of the campaign we were all hot on the trail of who was going to sue whom for slander, which candidate was carrying on with what mystery woman, and who was appealing to what ethnic group."

Borreca added that the media clearly missed the coming storm and financial crisis in the state in 1995.

Nevertheless, POP '94 ushered in a new era of greater political participation. Citizens' groups have grown in number and influence in recent years. They address issues from neighborhood concerns to Hawaiian sovereignty, demonstrating that a large and diverse number of island residents are concerned about their home. Organizations such as Nā Pua Ke Ali'i Pauahi, a nonprofit group that includes Kamehameha School students, faculty, teachers, parents and alumni, were at the forefront of late-1990s complaints about the management of the Bishop Estate. That effort generated huge media attention and suggested that the "status quo" very much needed to be challenged—and in radical ways. Roth's POP organization lay dormant during the 1996 elections but continued to hold weekly radio discussions on important issues, with viewpoints expressed in the Sunday *Advertiser*. By 1997 Roth had launched POPWEB, an Internet home page, and POP Accountability Project to follow up on campaign promises made by politicians.

Do such community initiatives and media-led political forums and advertisements help voters decide? How many voters even pay attention to them? There were more political messages in the 1994 and 1996 campaigns than in previous elections. The Hawaii Newspaper Agency, which publishes the *Advertiser* and the *Star-Bulletin*, reported heavier than expected campaign ads, most of them attributable to the 1994 special election for Honolulu mayor. KITV Channel 4 ran twice as many ads in 1994 as it did in 1992; as a result, local media offered more election-related news stories.

More news coverage and political advertisements do not necessarily mean that people—in the age of television sound bites—read and heard every word, let alone considered the issues. The potential, though, was there. Anyone who watched television or glanced at a newspaper could not avoid political messages. The question is whether that potential can or will be translated into political action. The rapid development of telecommunications offers the possibility, at minimum, of broader political participation that can lead to improvement of island society.

Building a Future

In the early 1970s, the "Hawaii State Commission on the Year 2000" was appointed by the governor's office to evaluate the islands' future. *Hawaii 2000: Continuing Experiment in Anticipatory Democracy* includes the observations and visions of many participants, mostly scholars and other professionals, in a Commission-sponsored conference. The conference attracted over 700 participants to Honolulu, including guests from abroad ("In our group were those of Hawaiian, Japanese, Chinese, Filipino, and Caucasian extraction," the editors wrote). Among the conference principles expressed were: support of top-level governmental officials, but not political domination by them; emphasis on local intellectual and organizational leadership; balancing efforts to contribute to global, national and intersocial viewpoints; and encouragement of diversified citizen participation. *Hawaii 2000* was nonbinding—that is, no specific proposals were implemented publicly or privately. Rather, consciousness-raising was the official intent. "The 'aloha spirit' is a basic ingredient of a style of life based on the essential equality and dignity of all human beings," wrote Douglas S. Yamamura and Harry V. Ball in *Hawaii 2000*. "The basic qualities of this way of life are perhaps best characterized by such terms as openness, hospitality, neighborly concern, tolerance, general acceptance of others, emotional warmth, genuine love for other people, and friendliness."

Other *Hawaii 2000* contributors concurred. "Perhaps more than in any state in the union, the citizens of Hawaii identify themselves together, bound by unique customs, music, geography, and dress," wrote John F. McDermott, Jr. But McDermott, writing in the early 1970s, did not believe complete acculturation and homogenization of the islands' various racial groups would come soon if at all; nor did he see the future free of conflict. "Rather, our ethnic groups will still retain their own identity, providing a series of balanced contrasts, and it is to be considered that the survival of these differences may be a source of cultural enrichment to be maintained.... One essential feature, however, will be the continued giving up by each group of a certain [amount] of its own cultural uniqueness in order to come together in a common commitment toward a shared 'Hawaiian' identity." Race relations were also on the minds of *Hawaii 2000* participants. "We believe," wrote Yamamura and Ball, "...that the problem of race is the preeminent social challenge of the twentieth century, that it has not been solved, and that it poses the fundamental threat to any orderly transition to a desirable future or futures—or even to any future."

Concerns about race relations were not unique to *Hawaii 2000*, for others have observed similar views. "The increasing disposition to concede that the millennium in race relations has not yet arrived in Hawaii and that behind the facade of perfection sometimes presented by public figures and advertising agents there are ordinary people with ordinary weaknesses and foibles is unquestionably one of the more significant advances towards greater realism in human relations which have been brought about in the period since Statehood," wrote Andrew W. Lind in *Hawaii: The Last of the Magic Isles*. "This reduction in the pretensions of inter-racial perfection should also help to eliminate the present danger that Hawaii might be called upon to validate its claim and to produce the magical formula." Whatever the reality, within the Hawai'i experiment in multicultural democracy, there is still great promise. Wrote Lawrence W. Fuchs in *Hawaii Pono*: "Hawaii illustrates the nation's revolutionary message of equality of opportunity for all, regardless of background, color, or religion. This is the promise of Hawaii, a promise for the entire nation and, indeed, the world, that peoples of different races and creeds can live together, enriching each other, in harmony and democracy."

University of Hawai'i scholar Paul F. Hooper noted in *Elusive Destiny* that Governor Jack Burns believed that the Hawai'i experience proved peoples of diverse backgrounds could live together successfully. "Hawaii's people are thoroughly American," Burns said. "More than this, they are American in an entirely unique way. Democracy, American democracy, is practiced in Hawaii as it is practiced nowhere else in the world.... The diverse makeup of Hawaii's people is a decided strength both in itself and as an example and a guide for all peoples.... Hawaii is living proof that peoples of all races, cultures and creeds can live together in harmony and well-being." For these reasons and others, Burns sought to forge an internationalist role for Hawai'i in the affairs of the Pacific Basin. He believed that Hawai'i's progressive economic, social and political structures—particularly multiracial harmony—could serve as an example to the world. But, while sympathetic to Burns' views, Hooper found them at odds with a generally pessimistic perception of people and society in the twentieth century. "In a world where terrorism, chauvinism, and hedonism are accepted and on occasion even praised, internationalist undertakings in the Hawaiian mode face undeniably bleak prospects," he wrote. "Indeed, it is likely that this pessimism has already had an effect. Despite persistent efforts at a serious portrayal of Hawaii, people elsewhere continue to view the Islands as little more than a glamorous playground. Few are aware of the deeper issues and fewer still care enough to take them seriously. Further, it may be that even the people of Hawaii are succumbing to this tendency." Hooper cited growing ethnic tension and an inability to translate paradisiacal ideals into action.

Others concur. "The truth of the matter is that ethnic tension in Hawaii is growing and a tradition of tolerance tends to mask this," wrote Franklin Odo and Susan Yim. They noted that part of this problem is due to mainland whites who move here expecting Hawai'i to be no different from anyplace else. These newcomers are not accustomed to the Asian or local influence and the extent to which whites do not wield dominant power. Meanwhile, in Hawai'i as elsewhere, Japanese Americans are suffering from the "model minority" stereotype so many ascribe to them. "Like any other group, they have crime, failure, and dysfunction," Odo and Yim explained. "This doesn't fit their image." They have also become targets of criticism by those who believe Japanese Americans control Hawai'i state and local government. "Every ethnic group has its own perspectives and concerns, but the case of the Japanese Americans is especially critical because they have dictated, in so many ways, the status quo," Odo and Yim argued. "If they feel threatened, they will respond by circling the wagons. Like most groups under siege, they will become defensive, protect their steadily diminishing areas of influence, and succumb to the temptation to use more nepotism rather than to become more egalitarian and inclusive." Because of their sizable population, the authors add, the impact of this fractionalization on the larger community could be considerable.

Scholar Elizabeth Wittermans wrote that the future of Hawai'i will likely bring both further purification and ethnic equality, but also a narrowing down of inter-ethnic relations. This will be marked by increased cooperation among communities but also sudden flare-ups of "old resentments," especially when social and economic positions are perceived as being threatened. However, Wittermans believed that pluralistic forces and a lack of educational and occupational constraints will cut across such trends. A critical element of this will be Hawai'i's pattern of racism, which is to disperse racist behavior rather than concentrate it. She labels this pattern "hopeful."

Others are less optimistic. "Some would argue that what happened in the former Yugoslavia, now Bosnia-Herzegovina, could never happen in Hawaii," wrote Cindy Kobayashi in the *Advertiser*. "However, a wise man has told me that Yugoslavia was a place where many thought 'it could never happen.' Hawaii has become a place where discrimination is a fact of life; the way in which we make choices on where we live, who we marry, where we send our children to school are all influenced by what we call 'local culture.' But speaking as one who has been brought up in one of the most closed ethnic groups in Hawaii [Japanese], I can honestly say that what is behind the mystique of 'local culture' is nothing but a plain old disgust for the 'Other.'"

The tendency to embrace one's own group is still quite evident in Hawai'i. For example, the April 21, 1995, cover of the *Hawaii Herald*, a Japanese-American periodical, featured what it called the "next generation" of politicians elected in 1994 to the state Legislature; however, the *Herald* listed only six young, Japanese-American men, even though dozens of people from several ethnic groups and a few women had been elected. The August 16-31, 1996, issue of the *Fil-Am Courier* ran a similar cover that featured only male, Filipino-American politicians in Hawai'i. Of course, the *Herald* and the *Courier* appeal to select audiences, but the line between selectivity and exclusion is thin. In a community that lays claim to racial egalitarianism, such selectivity may be viewed with suspicion. Hawai'i's diverse population gives it the unique potential to be the multicultural model of legend. But much work remains to be done to realize that potential.

Facing the Problems

Bob Stauffer wrote in the *Honolulu Weekly* that there will never be an equivalent of the so-called 1954 "revolution." Rather, change will be slow in coming, if it comes at all. Those who want change the most—those who have moved to Hawai'i from the mainland—are the least understanding of the importance of the events of 1954, especially to the island's Japanese population, which still has the highest proportion of state leaders. Even with retirements, Japanese will continue to replace Japanese. "Fully half of all votes today in Hawaii are cast by Japanese Americans, most of them as a bloc. No other ethnic group or interest group remotely approximates their power because the other groups aren't registered (half of the electorate is disenfranchised today by not being registered— and these non-registrants are not of Japanese ancestry), and even those who are registered either don't vote or don't vote as a bloc." Stauffer continued: "Try to remember a single time when a Japanese leader publicly attacked another Japanese leader here. Now consider the haoles and Hawaiians. Simply put, it is no accident that all 43 of George Ariyoshi's employees during his lengthy legislative career were Japanese. Or that three-fourths of his Cabinet when he left office was Japanese. Or why, even today, half of the Legislature, over half of the senior civil service, half of the memberships on boards and commissions and half of all government jobs and contracts go to Japanese Americans. This is again 'democracy' in a classic sense: One group casts half of the votes. They get half of the political returns. Simple."

The vast majority of island residents of Japanese ancestry, said Stauffer, own homes and saw their net worth increase an average of $200,000 per household over a three-year period in the late 1980s. They are thus enjoying both political and economic rewards and will not want to see that change, because "life is good ... the dream is still alive, still being fulfilled." Instead, "the electorate will continue to be purposely disenfranchised," predicted Stauffer. "We will continue not to be a democracy; change will come slowly; witty (usually malihini) haoles will continue to write articles showing how abusive the system is (thinking, and probably believing, that this means something); and kamaaina haoles and Hawaiians will continue to pine for the old days—or for sovereignty."

Former state legislator David Hagino worried that third- and fourth- generation Japanese males in Hawai'i feel left out of the political process today—especially in comparison to the *nisei*—noting that there are few prominent Japanese-American males in the state Legislature or the courts, though there are several prominent Japanese-American women in such positions. He suggested that this breeds resentment that may lead these males to support only Japanese male candidates in the future.

The story of Filipinos' empowerment is similar to that of the Japanese immigrants and their descendants in Hawai'i, and it may result not only in the elevation of a people but also yet another camp of exclusivity. Efforts by Filipino organizations to earn Filipino-American World War II veterans proper recognition and benefits is very similar to Japanese-American accomplishments in the same regard. There are more recent examples, as well. In an official visit to Hawai'i a year after the 1994 election, Philippine President Fidel Ramos met with Governor Cayetano, noting half in jest that the Philippines' productivity is becoming almost as good as its reproductivity. "And that's part of why Ben Cayetano probably got elected" as Hawai'i's first Filipino-American governor, Ramos joked to the *Advertiser*. Oceanic Cable added two Filipino channels to its lineup in 1995. The Mabuhay Channel is owned and managed by local Filipinos, with programming that includes a variety of topics from the Philippines, but mainly dedicated to Filipinos in Hawai'i. The other outlet is the Filipino Channel, which picks up a satellite feed directly from the Philippines. KITV Channel 4 scheduled a year-long series of special programs in 1995 designed to teach viewers the history, traditions, values and accomplishments of Hawai'i Filipinos. The programs' banner, "Bayanihan," takes its name from the communal work and activity of Filipino villagers at harvest time. The program ran into 1996, a year marking the 90th anniversary of the *sakada*, the arrival of the first Filipino immigrants to Hawai'i. KITV had previously produced similar series about Japanese and Chinese immigration to Hawai'i, as well as celebrated various Hawaiian cultural events.

"In this election, we are at a crossroads of deciding between being politically independent and merging with the mainstream but losing some bargaining power as a group, or voting as a bloc at the expense of compromising personal beliefs, friendships and loyalties," noted the editors of the *Hawaii Filipino Chronicle* shortly before the 1994 election. "Therein lies the voting dilemma of the Filipino voter." *MidWeek* columnist Dan Boylan observed that Filipinos will likely be as successful as the Japanese, but not for some time—and not ever unless they "get their act together and unite" as did Japanese Americans following World War II. But the desire is evident. "One's ethnic identity was clearly visible in physical features, customs, name and food," wrote UH scholar Leonard Y. Andaya of his experiences growing up in the islands. "I was a Filipino boy from Hawaii, and I was also an American. Being a product of the assimilationist philosophy of U.S. education, I was especially proud when Hawaii gained statehood in 1959 and became a full-fledged member of the union. As children of immigrants, we believed in the American dream and welcomed the opportunities which beckoned." Andaya called upon Filipinos in Hawai'i to rediscover their cultural roots and share in a Filipino heritage.

Is embracing one's ethnic group a celebration of culture or an obstacle to bettering relations with others? Do historic patterns invariably lead to a rejection of others? That is the debate. "There is no middle ground," said writer Tom Marks. "Either we are going to come together, or we are going to stand apart in Balkan-like fashion.... Either we are a multi-ethnic, multiracial community—which has in every sense mingled— its bloodlines as well as its cultures—or we are something sectarian which seeks to exalt one trace of lineage over another for ideological reasons." Marks added that sovereignty as articulated by some is designed to counter the "sectarian dominance of Western, haole culture." That path leads away from tolerance, which he viewed as the essence of cultures that have shaped Hawai'i. Jill Center, a white student at Kaimukī High School in the mid-1990s, recently transferred from Washington, D.C., wrote the *Advertiser*, "At my school there is more racism than I have ever seen before.... At lunch,

Japanese sit in one section, Hawaiians sit in another, Filipinos sit in their own section and so forth." She noted the ways in which Hawai'i grapples with its race-related problems, including through humor, private discussions and safety in numbers. These help diffuse tension but do not constructively address a growing problem. A California native, Center was concerned that people in Hawai'i do not talk openly or directly about race relations. "Each of us must start talking about race," she wrote. "If we do not start talking, the consequences could be bleak."

Al Miles wrote in *Honolulu* magazine that even though Hawai'i does not have crosses burning in people's yards or frequent drive-by shootings in inner-city Honolulu, racism does indeed exist. Miles challenged several myths about race relations in the islands. Most racism is not necessarily directed against whites, he wrote, but to many whites it seems so because they have been used to a unique position of entitlement. All racial stereotypes are not created equal, for the more hostile stereotypes usually refer to darker-skinned people such as Filipinos, Samoans, Hawaiians and blacks. Some people actually believe there is no racism in Hawai'i because of tolerance or the *aloha* spirit. "Until we finally acknowledge that the problem of racism exists in Hawaii, and begin speaking openly about the issues that confront us as a result, we will continue to do harm to ourselves," Miles declared.

Local periodicals increasingly feature such articles on race relations in the islands. The *Advertiser*, for example, featured a "Focus" section on the topic, "Are We All Getting Along?" (The precedent for such publications was perhaps set during a 1934 visit by President Franklin D. Roosevelt, when the *Star-Bulletin* published a special "progress" edition that reported on many aspects of Hawaiian society.) An accompanying editorial stressed that group harmony was the state's "greatest asset" and cited a poll that asked what people thought of the statement, "In Hawaii, people of different ethnic and racial backgrounds get along better than almost anywhere else." Over 83 percent of those polled agreed. The poll did not ask, but the same people might also acknowledge that most residents *do* hold racial and ethnic preferences and that these preferences profoundly influence island society—and that there is a fine line between "preferences" and prejudice. While many— perhaps most—Hawai'i residents would freely acknowledge their "preference" for people like themselves, few would call themselves prejudiced. But what do they say at the polls? Hawai'i's political structure reflects voter support for the notions that some ethnic and racial groups *are* superior to other groups, that to the rich *belongs* the power and that women are *not* the equal of men. Few would openly subscribe to such views, but that is the message that emerges from Hawai'i politics today.

In a sense, such a view is uncomplicated and easily perpetuated. Perhaps that is one reason the issue of gay rights so upsets island residents, for it represents a radical challenge to the status quo. But such a structure is a *terrible* limitation of human potential. It rules out the needed participation of groups long under-represented. It denies *every* voter the critical opportunity of choosing leaders based on the power of their ideas, experience and character rather than their physical qualities. It prevents the people of Hawai'i from having the *best* government—and thus the *best* society—a diverse people can aspire to. When Hawaiians are dying, when women and children are beaten and killed, when the poor face a future of no hope, then Hawai'i's politics have failed. Surely the promise of Hawai'i is greater than this.

Fulfilling the Promise

Hawai'i must work to establish a true multiparty system, for the dominance of one party—while a benign one—at minimum dictates that only certain voices will ever be heard. "We don't envision taking over the government," stated James M. Rath, a Republican County Councilman representing North

Kona. "We have no desire to replace one machine with another. We are working toward a true two-party system. I feel about a 50-50 mix would be enough to keep all the crooks, thieves, and charlatans in check!" Change will be difficult, for public cynicism about government reached an all-time high in the 1990s. Four out of five Hawai'i voters believed the Kenneth Rappolt case, in which a Honolulu official tied a nonbid contract to political campaign donations, was typical of the way business is done in both city and state government. But this certainly is not the best that Hawai'i politics can aspire to. Even a roughly balanced two-party system permits the voter an alternative. That alternative does not presently exist.

This leads to another point: campaign finance practice must be reformed. Nearly 60 percent of those polled by the *Advertiser* believed that political contributions from those who get nonbid contracts from government should be banned. "Suppliers and potential suppliers to the state are 'requested' to make donations when it goes without saying that a failure to donate will be conspicuous," observed *Honolulu Weekly*'s Robert M. Rees. "Yet we accept this intimidation and even wink at each other about our 'contributions.' We accept too easily that 75 percent of the governor's campaign contributions have come from state suppliers awarded jobs on a noncompetitive and sole-source basis." Rees believed many public employees work at their jobs in silence rather than risk criticizing the state government.

"Our elections are overdosing on special-interest money, and this isn't just between the candidates and their contributors," explained Larry Meacham of Common Cause, a citizen advocacy group. "Every dollar of special-interest contributions to a candidate results in big hidden costs to the taxpayer." Meacham said that special-interest contributions, such as those from nonbid contractors, are small down-payments so that politicians will do favors for big money once in office. Nonbid contractors and other special-interest contributors are only part of the overall campaign-finance picture, however. Meacham has called for reforms that would limit campaign contributions and identify the employers of those who contribute large sums of money. He would also like to see public financing of campaigns. "That's the ultimate answer," he said. "Since the taxpayers are paying anyway, why not pay $1 now rather than $100 or $1,000 after the election? Until we clean up this dirty system, the politicians will continue to obey the special interests."

At least one political party does not accept funds from political action committees and large corporations. "Campaigns should be financed by the people, not by special interests or corporations," explained Ira Rohter, co-chair of Hawai'i's Green Party. "The debt of elected officials should be to the people of Hawaii, not to big contributors." As of this writing, however, the Green Party has succeeded only in electing a few officials.

A State Government News report showed Hawai'i's candidates in 1994 spent more money per voter than those in any other state. "It's clear to me that a lot of money was wasted," said Larry Meacham. "The only people who benefit from this huge amount of spending is the TV stations." *Honolulu* magazine writer Bob Dye noted that loopholes in existing laws permit bundling of contributions—that is, making a campaign contribution beyond the legal limit by donating funds, goods or services in the names of others, such as family members or coworkers. "Bundling tilts the field in favor of high spenders and corrupts elected officials," said Dye. "Bundled money supports extravagant political lifestyles. Worse, bundled money is added onto project costs, and ends up being paid by taxpayers. But saddest of all, bundled-money donors buy big-time power, making manini [trivial] your vote and mine." Dye believes the Legislature should close the loopholes that permit bundled contributions.

Candidates and contributors seeking to evade campaign contribution limits have proved to be creative. Dan Boylan noted that politicians such as Pat Saiki and Arnold Morgado have received loans that far exceed the legal limits of campaign contributions, even though these "loans" will likely never be paid back. Other candidates disguise the source of contributions. *Star-Bulletin* journalist Ian Lind explained that the "laundering" of money to campaigns, though illegal, is widespread. One method is a variation on bundling wherein a donor presents an envelope of cash to a campaign treasurer along with a list of names of "fellow" donors; the real donor, often a single developer or a corporation, thus is able to exceed the legal individual contribution level. The candidate may know that an individual "raised" this money on the candidate's behalf, but the candidate usually does not know precisely where the money came from. Frank Fasi, for example, often received donations of $25,000 or more through this practice, according to Lind.

Another method is for the owner of a business (or, more discreetly, the owner's secretaries or office director) to ask employees to make a donation to a campaign from their business expense accounts. The money thus appears to come from an individual but in fact comes from the business. It is no coincidence, then, when these same businesses are awarded nonbid contracts by the elected official who received the campaign donations. The state's Campaign Spending Commission does not computerize these records and only occasionally makes them available to the public, said Lind, because the commission is not required by law to do so. When such reports are made available, they are usually only summaries of the major contributions. It is thus difficult for the media or others to obtain a detailed list of campaign donations and their sources.

In Hawai'i, donations can be carried over to elections other than the one for which the donation was initially made (this is not permitted at the federal level). This explains why the "Friends of Fasi" committee, for example, has raised such an immense amount of money for Fasi over many years (legally, Fasi cannot draw on this money unless he runs for office). The state Legislature has debated campaign-finance reform, including the possibility of following federal law that corporations and unions cannot contribute directly to a campaign, but must instead form a political action committee to solicit money and keep it separate from their own treasuries. But, as of this writing, only minor measures that do not address the larger problem have been enacted. "There has been little political will to enforce the laws that we have," said Lind. "We don't so much need to revise the existing laws as we need to make the Campaign Spending Commission does its job to enforce the statutes that are there. This hasn't been done because those with the legislative power want to keep it the way it is, presumably because they benefit from this."

Establishment of a multiparty system and finance reform are the two most important steps toward fulfilling the promise of Hawai'i, but Hawai'i might also consider changing the structure of its state government. *Star-Bulletin* columnist A.A. Smyser has suggested that multimember districts be reinstated by constitutional convention in order to diversify representation. In 1982, the Legislature's Reapportionment Committee eliminated multimember districts in favor of single-member districts, a move that many in office are comfortable with as it solidifies their support base. Former state Senator Mary George said that Republicans committed "political suicide" when they agreed to the switch to single-member districts. "In a single-member district the party in power controls the drawing of district boundaries, so you can outnumber your enemies by the way you draw a district or put them all in one district so they only have one representative," she said. "You cannot talk about ethnic dominance in politics without thinking of these differences."

Others, including Dan Boylan, have suggested giving Hawai'i a unicameral Legislature. Replacing the current House and Senate with a single body could reduce government expense as well as streamline representation. Having 51 representatives and 27 senators is too much representation for a state with barely a million population. (Nebraska, which is slightly larger than Hawai'i in population, is the only state in the country with a unicameral Legislature.) Robert M. Rees has suggested that the state's legislative session be extended as a way to make government more effective. Hawai'i has one of the shortest legislative sessions in the nation.

Such changes will not come easily because those in power are not likely to alter the mechanisms which put them in power, let alone relinquish their positions altogether. Besides, many of these leaders believe they are doing what is best for Hawai'i, that they *are* the righteous descendants of the '54 revolution that elevated a long-oppressed people. Ironically, this attitude differs little from that of the plantation owners and Republicans who thought what *they* did was best for Hawai'i. Today, as before 1954, the voices and needs of many—including women, gays and the poor—are not being heard.

A new political machine will not empower those voices. Rather, all of Hawai'i must work hard to listen to and include all of its citizens in the political process. At the same time, individuals must assume their own responsibility and pay attention to politicians and their platforms, rather than vote on face value or name recognition—or not vote at all. Voters who take the trouble to inform themselves about individual candidates and issues are less likely to vote along party or ethnic (or other irrelevant) lines, and Hawai'i could find itself embracing a true multiparty system at last. Such voters are also less likely to reelect officials who evade campaign-finance rules, whether or not the Legislature enacts meaningful reform.

Democracy is an ongoing process. One election or politician will not change everything overnight. Rather, each election can and should be a necessary step toward the betterment of society. This is the promise of democracy, and therein lies the promise of Hawai'i and its people. Hawai'i is not a multicultural utopia, but it does hold a diverse population that lives in relative harmony in spite of great problems. At their best, these people work to better their society rather than retreat into separate camps. Such a principle can be applied directly to the arena of Hawai'i politics—by each and every citizen.

References

"1995 Hawaii Kids Count Data Book." Unpublished document. Honolulu: University of Hawaii Center on the Family, the Governor's Office of Children and Youth and the Hawaii Community Services Council, 1995.

Agbayani, Amefil R. "Community Impacts of Migration: Recent Ilokano Migration to Hawaii." *Social Process in Hawaii*, 33 (1991), 73-90.

_____. Interview. Honolulu, March 13, 1995.

Alegado, Dean T. "The Filipino Community in Hawaii: Development and Change." *Social Process in Hawaii*, 33 (1991), 12-38.

_____. "Voter Turnout for November 4, 1994." Photocopied. Honolulu: University of Hawaii Ethnic Studies Program, November 1994.

_____. Interview. Honolulu, April 18, 1995.

Allen, Gwenfread E. "Caucasian Women in Hawaii." In "Montage: An Ethnic History of Women in Hawaii," eds. Nancy Foo Young and Judy R. Parrish, 21-29. Honolulu: General Assistance Center for the Pacific, College of Education, Educational Foundation, University of Hawai'i and State Commission on the Status of Women, 1977.

Anderson, Robert N., Richard Coller and Rebecca F. Pestano. Filipinos in Rural Hawaii. Honolulu: University of Hawaii Press, 1984.

Aoudé, Ibrahim G. "Hawaii: The Housing Crisis and the State's Development Strategy." *Social Process in Hawaii*, 35 (1994), 71-84.

Aquino, Belinda A. "Filipino Women Workers in Hawaii." Filipinas, 1 (1980), 81-96.

Bailey, Beth, and David Farber. *The First Strange Place: The Alchemy of Race and Sex in World War II Hawaii.* New York: Free Press, 1992.

Bank of Hawaii. "Hawaii 1994: Annual Economic Report, Vol. 44." Economics Department. Honolulu: December 1994.

Baro, Agnes L. "Effective Political Control of Bureaucracy: The Case of Hawaii's Prison System." Unpublished Doctoral Dissertation, Sam Houston State University, 1991.

Barringer, Herbert, and Patricia O'Hagan. "Socioeconomic Characteristics of Native Hawaiians." Honolulu: Alu Like, Inc., 1989.

Beechert, Edward D. "The Political Economy of Hawaii and Working Class Consciousness." *Social Process in Hawaii*, 31 (1984), 155-181.

_____. *Working in Hawaii: A Labor History.* Honolulu: University of Hawaii Press, 1985.

Bell, Bella Zi, Eleanor C. Nordyke, and Patricia O'Hagan. "Fertility and Maternal and Child Health." *Social Process in Hawaii*, 32 (1989), 87-103.

Blair, Robert Chad. "Democracy in Hawaii: Class, Race and Gender in Local Politics." Unpublished Doctoral Dissertation, University of Hawai'i, 1996.

Blaisdell, Kekuni. "Historical and Cultural Aspects of Native Hawaiian Health." *Social Process in Hawaii*, 32 (1989), 1-21.

Boylan, Dan. "Blood Runs Thick: Ethnicity as a Factor in Hawaii's Politics." In *Politics and Public Policy in Hawaii*, eds. Richard C. Pratt and Zachary A. Smith, 67-80. Albany: State University of New York Press, 1992.

_____. "Crosscurrents: Filipinos in Hawaii's Politics." *Social Process in Hawaii*, 33 (1991), 39-55.

_____. Interview. Honolulu, November 22, 1994.

Burris, Jerry. "Has Hawaii Been Hurt by Cronyism in Government?" In *The Price of Paradise: Volume II*, ed. Randall W. Roth, 289-292. Honolulu: Mutual Publishing, 1993.

_____. Interview. Honolulu, March 23, 1995.

Caces, Maria Fe F. "Personal Networks and the Material Adaptation of Recent Immigrants: A Study of Filipinos in Hawaii." Unpublished Doctoral Dissertation, University of Hawai'i, 1985.

Chang, Deborah. "Power, Politics, and Powerlessness: Kohala People and Their Future." *Social Process in Hawaii*, 27 (1979), 116-128.

Chaplin, George. *Presstime in Paradise: The Life and Times of The Honolulu Advertiser*. Honolulu: University of Hawai'i Press, 1997.

Chaplin, George, and Glenn D. Paige, eds. *Hawaii 2000: Continuing Experiment in Anticipatory Democracy*. Honolulu: University Press of Hawaii, 1973.

Char, Walter F., Wen-shing Tseng, Kwong-Yen Lum, and Jing Hsu. "The Chinese." In *Peoples and Cultures of Hawaii: A Psychocultural Profile*, eds. John T. McDermott, Jr., Wen-shing Tseng, and Thomas W. Maretzki, 53-72. Honolulu: John A. Burns School of Medicine and The University Press of Hawaii, 1980.

Chinen, Joyce. "Internationalization of Capital, Migration, Reindustrialization, and Women Workers in the Garment Industry." *Social Process in Hawaii*, 35 (1994), 85-102.

Chou, Michaelyn Pi-hsia. "The Education of a Senator: Hiram L. Fong, from 1906 to 1954." Unpublished Doctoral Dissertation, University of Hawai'i, 1980.

Coffman, Tom. *Catch a Wave: A Case Study of Hawaii's New Politics*. Honolulu: University Press of Hawaii, 1973.

_____. Interview. Kāne'ohe, November 23, 1994.

Cooper, George, and Gavan Daws. *Land and Power in Hawaii: The Democratic Years*. Honolulu: Benchmark Books, Honolulu 1985.

Correa, Genevieve, and Edgar C. Knowlton, Jr. "The Portuguese in Hawaii." *Social Process in Hawaii*, 29 (1982), 70-77.

Crowningburg-Amalu, Samuel. *Jack Burns: A Portrait in Transition*. Honolulu: Mamalahoa Foundation, 1974.

Daly, Bill. Interview. Honolulu, July 6, 1995.

Daws, Gavan. *Shoal of Time: A History of the Hawaiian Islands*. New York: Macmillan Company, 1968.

Day, A. Grove. *Hawaii: Fiftieth Star*. New York: Duell, Sloan and Pearce, 1960.

"Domestic Violence Jury Trial backlog: A Report from the Domestic Violence Coordinating Council." Unpublished document. Submitted to the Seventeenth Legislature in response to House Resolution 410-93. Honolulu: State Center for Alternative Dispute Resolution, 1993.

Farrell, Bryan H. *Hawaii, the Legend that Sells*. Honolulu: University of Hawaii Press, 1982.

Fil-Am Courier. Honolulu: 1994-1996.

Fitisemanu, Diana, et al. "Family Dynamics Among Pacific Islander Americans." *Social Process in Hawaii*, 36 (1994), 26-40.

Forman, Sheila M. "Filipino Participation in Civil Rights Policies and Practices in Hawaii." *Social Process in Hawaii*, 33 (1991), 1-11.

_____. "Hawaii's Immigrants from the Philippines." In *Peoples and Cultures of Hawaii: A Psychocultural Profile*, eds. John T. McDermott, Jr., Wen-shing Tseng, and Thomas W. Maretzki, 163-178. Honolulu: John A. Burns School of Medicine and The University Press of Hawaii, 1980.

Freedman, Chuck. "Can You Name the Big Five?" In *The Price of Paradise: Volume II*, ed. Randall W. Roth, 79-85. Honolulu: Mutual Publishing, 1993.

Fuchs, Lawrence H. *Hawaii Pono: A Social History*. New York: Harcourt Brace Jovanovich, Publishers, 1961.

"General Welfare Summary." Unpublished document. Honolulu: POP '94, 1994.

George, Mary. Interview. Kailua, Hawai'i, March 7, 1995.

Geschwender, James A. "Lessons from Waiahole-Waikane." *Social Process in Hawaii*, 28 (1980-81), 121-135.

Glenn, Evelyn Nakano. *Issei, Nisei, War Bride: Three Generations of Japanese American Women in Domestic Service*. Philadelphia: Temple University Press, 1986.

_____. "Occupational Ghettoization: Japanese American Women and Domestic Service, 1905-1970." Boston: Department of Sociology, Boston University, 1979.

Grant, Glen. Interview. Honolulu, March 23, 1995.

Gray, Francine du Plessix. *Hawaii: The Sugar-Coated Fortress*. New York: Vintage Books, 1972.

Griffin, John. "Is Hawaii Unique?" In *The Price of Paradise: Volume II*, ed. Randall W. Roth, 73-77. Honolulu: Mutual Publishing, 1993.

Grimshaw, Patricia. "New England Missionary Wives, Hawaiian Women, and 'The Cult of True Womanhood.'" *Hawaiian Journal of History*, 19 (1985), 71-100.

Haas, Michael. "Comparing Paradigms of Ethnic Politics in the United States: The Case of Hawaii." Western Political Quarterly, 40:4 (December 1987), 647-672.

_____. *Institutional Racism: The Case of Hawaii.* Westport, Connecticut: Praeger, 1992.

Haas, Michael, and Peter P. Resurrection, eds. *Politics and Prejudice in Contemporary Hawaii.* Honolulu: Coventry Press, 1976.

Hagino, David. "Palaka Power." Photocopied. Honolulu: 1979.

_____. Interview. Honolulu, May 30, 1995.

Harwell, Jay. *Na Mamo: Hawaiian People Today,* Honolulu: Pohaku Press, 1996.

Hawaii Business. Honolulu: September 1993-May 1998.

Hawaii Commission on the Status of Women. "Domestic Violence Report." Honolulu: State of Hawaii, 1993.

Hawaii Department of Business, Economic Development and Tourism (DBEDT). "1990 Census Tract Names for the State of Hawaii." Information Resources Management Division. Honolulu: June 1994.

_____. "City and County of Honolulu: Facts and Figures 1994." Research and Economic Analysis Division. Honolulu: 1994.

_____. "County of Hawaii: Facts and Figures 1994." Research and Economic Analysis Division. Honolulu: 1994.

_____. "General Population and Housing Characteristics for the State of Hawaii: 1990." Information Resources Management Division, Hawaii State Data Center Report Number 6. Honolulu: July 1993.

_____. "General Social and Economic Characteristics for the State of Hawaii: 1990." Information Resources Management Division, Hawaii State Data Center Report Number 8. Honolulu: November 1994.

_____. "Profile of Rural Hawaii: A Look at Demographic, Economic and Social Trends in Rural Hawaii." Honolulu: May 1994.

_____. "State of Hawaii: Facts and Figures 1994." Research and Economic Analysis Division. Honolulu: 1994.

_____. "Statistical & Economic Report, State of Hawaii: 3rd Quarter 1994." Research and Economic Analysis Division. Honolulu: 1994.

_____. "The State of Hawaii Data Book 1993-94: A Statistical Abstract." Research and Economic Analysis Division. Honolulu: June 1994.

Hawaii Department of Health. "Biennial Report for 1991 and 1992: Vital Statistics Supplement." Office of Health Status Monitoring. Honolulu: August 1994.

Hawaii Filipino Chronicle. Honolulu: January-December 1994.

Hawaii Herald. Honolulu: January 1994-November 1995.

Hawaii Observer. Honolulu: January 1974-December 1976.

Hawaii Office of the Lieutenant Governor. "Electoral Boundary Descriptions." Election Services Division. Honolulu: 1994.

_____. "Precinct Boundary Descriptions." Election Services Division. Honolulu: 1994.

_____. "The Reapportionment and Redistricting of Legislative and Congressional Districts for the State of Hawaii as Adopted by the 1991 Reapportionment Commission." Election Services Division. Honolulu: 1991.

_____. "State of Hawaii Election Map, Representative Districts: 1st - 51st." Election Services Division. Honolulu: 1994.

_____. "Statement of Votes for the Offices of Governor and Lieutenant Governor, 1994." Election Services Division. Honolulu: 1994.

_____. "Statewide Summary Report for the 1994 General Election." Election Services Division. Honolulu: 1994.

_____. "Statewide Summary Report for the 1994 Primary Election." Election Services Division. Honolulu: 1994.

Hawaii Tribune Herald. Hilo, Hawaii: September and November 1994.

"Hawaii Women's Directory." Honolulu: Rainbow Bridge Consultants, 1995.

Hirono, Mazie. Interview. Honolulu, May 16, 1995.

Hiura, Arnold. Interview. Honolulu, June 2, 1995.

Honolulu. Honolulu: January 1994-May 1998.

The Honolulu Advertiser. Honolulu: September 1993-May 1998.

The Honolulu Star-Bulletin. Honolulu: September 1993-May 1998.

Honolulu Weekly. Honolulu: September 1993-May 1998.

Hooper, Paul F. *Elusive Destiny: The Internationalist Movement in Modern Hawaii.* Honolulu: University Press of Hawaii, 1980.

Hooper, Paul F., Daniel B. Boylan, and Stuart Gerry Brown. "John A. Burns Oral History Project." 31 sound cassettes accompanied by transcript. Honolulu: University of Hawaii, 1975.

Hopkins, Jerry, ed. "Frank DeLima's Joke Book." Honolulu: Bess Press, 1991.

Hori, Joan. "Japanese Prostitution in Hawaii During the Immigration Period." *Hawaiian Journal of History,* 15 (1981), 113-124.

Hormann, Bernhard L. "The Haoles." *Social Process in Hawaii,* 29 (1982), 32-44.

_____. "The Mixing Process." *Social Process in Hawaii*, 29 (1982), 116-129.

_____. "Selections from 'The Caucasian Minority.'" *Social Process in Hawaii*, 27 (1979), 28-37.

Hughes, Judith Gething. "Changes in the Legal Status." In "The Changing Lives of Hawaii's Women: Progress Since Statehood," ed. Ruth Lieben, 36-37. Honolulu: Foundation for Hawaii Women's History, 1985.

Ikeda, Kiyoshi. "Demographic Profile of Native Hawaiians: 1980-1986." Honolulu: University of Hawaii Department of Sociology. Undated.

Iwasa, Henry. Interview. Honolulu, March 9, 1995.

Joesting, Edward. *Hawaii: An Uncommon History*. New York: W.W. Norton & Company, Inc., 1972.

Johnson, David B. "An Overview of Ethnicity and Health in Hawaii." *Social Process in Hawaii*, 32 (1989), 67-86.

Johnson, Donald D., and Michael F. Miller. *Hawaii's Own: A History of the Hawaii Government Employees Association, AFSCME Local 152, AFL-CIO, 1934-1984*. Honolulu: HGEA, 1986.

Junasa, Bienvenido D. "Filipino Experience in Hawaii." *Social Process in Hawaii*, 29 (1982), 95-104.

Kaleiwahea, Wendy. "Profile of registered voters in Hawaii, February 1995." Unpublished, untitled report. Honolulu: Voter Contact Services, 1995 (Wendy Kaleiwahea provided this information to the author on behalf of Honolulu's Voter Contact Services).

_____. VCS Journal, Volume 8, Number 3. Voter Contact Services: Honolulu, early-1990s.

_____. VCS Journal, Volume 9, Number 1. Voter Contact Services: Honolulu, early-1990s.

Kamauu, Mahealani, and H.K. Bruss Keppeler. "What Might Sovereignty Look Like?" In *The Price of Paradise: Volume II*, ed. Randall W. Roth, 295-300. Honolulu: Mutual Publishing, 1993.

Kanahele, George S. "The New Hawaiians." *Social Process in Hawaii*, 29 (1982), 21-31.

Kassebaum, Gene. "Ethnicity and the Disposition of Arrests for Violent Crime in Honolulu." *Social Process in Hawaii*, 28 (1980-81), 33-57.

Kelley, Lane, and William Remus. "A Comparative Study of Occupational Success of Young Asian American Business Professionals in Hawaii." *Social Process in Hawaii*, 28 (1980-81), 58-72.

Kent, Noel J. *Hawaii: Islands Under the Influence.* New York: Monthly Review Press, 1983.

_____. "The End of the American Age of Abundance: Whither Hawaii?" *Social Process in Hawaii,* 35 (1994), 179-194.

_____. "Myth of the Golden Men: Ethnic Elites and Dependent Development in the 50th State." In *Ethnicity and Nation-Building in the Pacific,* ed. Michael C. Howard, 98-117. New York: United Nations University, 1989.

_____. "Straws in the Wind." *Social Process in Hawaii,* 31 (1984), 183-186.

Kim, Elaine H., and Janice Otani. *With Silk Wings: Asian American Women at Work.* Oakland, California: Asian Women United, 1983.

Kim, Karl. "The Political Economy of Foreign Investment in Hawaii." *Social Process in Hawaii,* 35 (1994), 40-55.

Kimura, Hubert S. *Aikane-to-Aikane: An Introduction to Grass-Roots Campaigning in Hawaii.* Honolulu: Hubert S. and Katherine J. Kimura, 1979.

_____. *The Akamai Strategist.* Honolulu: Hubert S. and Katherine J. Kimura, 1982.

Kirkpatrick, John. "Ethnic Antagonism and Innovation in Hawaii." In *Ethnic Conflict: International Perspectives,* eds. Jerry Boucher, Dan Landis, and Karen Arnold Clark, 298-316. Newbury Park, California: SAGE Publications, Inc., 1987.

Kometani, Franklin. Interview. Honolulu, March 8, 1995.

Krauss, Bob. *Johnny Wilson: First Hawaiian Democrat.* Honolulu: University of Hawaii Press, 1994.

Lau, Cori. "Should Same-sex Couples be Allowed to Marry?" In *The Price of Paradise: Volume II,* ed. Randall W. Roth, 231-237. Honolulu: Mutual Publishing, 1993.

Lebra, Joyce Chapman. *Women's Voices in Hawaii.* Niwot, Colorado: University Press of Colorado, 1991.

Ledesma, Bernadette Suguitan. "The Filipinos: The People Who Came and Stayed." In "A Legacy of Diversity: Contributions of the Hawaiians, Chinese, Japanese, Portuguese, Puerto Ricans, Koreans, Filipinos and Samoans in Hawaii," 81-91. Honolulu: Ethnic Resource Center for the Pacific, College of Education, Educational Foundations, University of Hawaii, 1975.

Lee, Anne F., and Linda Nishigaya. "Running and Winning." In "The Changing Lives of Hawaii's Women: Progress Since Statehood," ed. Ruth Lieben, 18-19. Honolulu: Foundation for Hawaii Women's History, 1985.

"A Legacy of Diversity: Contributions of the Hawaiians, Chinese, Japanese, Portuguese, Puerto Ricans, Koreans, Filipinos and Samoans in Hawaii." Honolulu: Ethnic Resource Center for the Pacific, College of Education, Educational Foundations, University of Hawaii, 1975.

Lewin, Jack. Interview. Honolulu, March 20, 1995.

Lieban, Ruth, ed. "The Changing Lives of Hawaii's Women: Progress Since Statehood." Honolulu: Foundation for Hawaii Women's History, 1985.

Lind, Andrew W. "Immigration to Hawaii." *Social Process in Hawaii*, 29 (1982), 9-20.

_____. "Race and Ethnic Relations: An Overview." *Social Process in Hawaii*, 29 (1982), 130-150.

_____. *Hawaii: The Last of the Magic Isles*. London: Oxford University Press, 1969.

_____. *Hawaii's People*. Honolulu: University of Hawaii Press, 1967.

Lind, Ian. Interview. Honolulu, March 27, 1995.

Luter, John. "In Newspaper and Magazines." In "The Changing Lives of Hawaii's Women: Progress Since Statehood," ed. Ruth Lieben, 34-35. Honolulu: Foundation for Hawaii Women's History, 1985.

Lynde, Allison H. "A Race for the Hawaii State House of Representatives, 1970: Strategies, Outcomes, and Interpretations." Unpublished Masters Thesis, University of Hawaii, 1970.

Maretzki, Thomas W., and John F. McDermott, Jr. "The Caucasians." In *Peoples and Cultures of Hawaii: A Psychocultural Profile*, eds. John T. McDermott, Jr., Wen-shing Tseng, and Thomas W. Maretzki, 25-52. Honolulu: John A. Burns School of Medicine and The University Press of Hawaii, 1980.

Mast, Robert H., and Anna B. Mast. *Autobiography of Protest in Hawaii*. Honolulu: University of Hawai'i Press, 1997.

Matayoshi, Coralie Chun. "Do Women in Hawaii Have Equal Access to Jobs?" In *The Price of Paradise: Lucky We Live Hawaii?* ed. Randall W. Roth, 205-209. Honolulu: Mutual Publishing, 1992.

McClain, David, Robert M. Rees, and Charles H. Turner. "Have Labor Unions Outlived Their Usefulness in Hawaii?" In *The Price of Paradise: Volume II*. ed. Randall W. Roth, 21-26. Honolulu: Mutual Publishing, 1993.

McClaren, John C. "Have We Left the Plantation Era?" In *The Price of Paradise: Volume II*, ed. Randall W. Roth, 217-222. Honolulu: Mutual Publishing, 1993.

McDermott, John F., Jr. "The Quality of Personal Life 2000." In *Hawaii 2000: Continuing Experiment in Anticipatory Democracy*, eds. George Chaplin and Glenn D. Paige, 162-175. Honolulu: University Press of Hawaii, 1973.

McDermott, John T., Jr., Wen-shing Tseng, and Thomas W. Maretzki, eds. *Peoples and Cultures of Hawaii: A Psychocultural Profile*. Honolulu: John A. Burns School of Medicine and The University Press of Hawaii, 1980.

_____. "Toward an Interethnic Society." In *Peoples and Cultures of Hawaii: A Psychocultural Profile*, eds. John T. McDermott, Jr., Wen-shing Tseng, and Thomas W. Maretzki, 225-232. Honolulu: John A. Burns School of Medicine and The University Press of Hawaii, 1980.

Meller, Norman. "The Legislative Party Profile in Hawaii." In "Papers of Hawaiian Politics 1952-1966," ed. Daniel W. Tuttle, Jr., 107-113. Honolulu: Hawaii State Program in Political Parties, 1966.

Meller, Norman, and Daniel W. Tuttle, Jr. "Hawaii: The Aloha State." In "Papers of Hawaiian Politics 1952-1966," ed. Daniel W. Tuttle, Jr., 67-97. Honolulu: Hawaii State Program in Political Parties, 1966.

Mengel, Laurie M. "Issei Women and Divorce in Hawai'i, 1885-1908." In Women in Hawai'i: Sites, Identities, and Voices, eds. Joyce N. Chinen, Kathleen O. Kane and Ida M. Yoshinaga, 18-37. Honolulu: University of Hawai'i Press, 1997.

MidWeek. Honolulu: September 1993-February 1998.

Miller, Michael F. "In Unions." In "The Changing Lives of Hawaii's Women: Progress Since Statehood," ed. Ruth Lieben, 31-33. Honolulu: Foundation for Hawaii Women's History, 1985.

Min, Sarrahm C-K. *Hawaii Without Hawaiians with Little Japan*. Honolulu: Still-Small-Voice-Press, 1979.

Miyasaki, Gail Y. "Contributions of Japanese Women in Hawaii." In "Montage: An Ethnic History of Women in Hawaii," eds. Nancy Foo Young and Judy R. Parrish, 45-49. Honolulu: General Assistance Center for the Pacific, College of Education, Educational Foundation, University of Hawaii, and State Commission on the Status of Women, 1977.

_____. "Contributions of the Japanese People to Hawaii." In "A Legacy of Diversity: Contributions of the Hawaiians, Chinese, Japanese, Portuguese, Puerto Ricans, Koreans, Filipinos and Samoans in Hawaii," 29-40. Honolulu: Ethnic Resource Center for the Pacific, College of Education, Educational Foundations, University of Hawaii, 1975.

Miwa, Ralph M. "Political Decision-making and the Law 2000." In *Hawaii 2000: Continuing Experiment in Anticipatory Democracy*, eds. George Chaplin and Glenn D. Paige, 214-233. Honolulu: University Press of Hawaii, 1973.

Nagtalon-Miller, Helen R. "Hawaii's Filipino Women." In "The Changing Lives of Hawaii's Women: Progress Since Statehood," ed. Ruth Lieben, 44-45. Honolulu: Foundation for Hawaii Women's History, 1985.

Nautu, Dorri, and Paul Spickard. "Ethnic Images and Social Distance Among Pacific Islanders in Hawaii." *Social Process in Hawaii*, 27 (1979), 70-87.

Nordyke, Eleanor C. *The Peopling of Hawaii*. Honolulu: University of Hawaii Press, 1989.

O'Connor, Dennis, Chair. "Democratic Party of Hawaii Platform." Unpublished pamphlet. Honolulu: May 1992.

Odo Franklin, and Susan Yim. "Are Race Relations in Hawaii Getting Better or Worse?" In *The Price of Paradise: Volume II*, ed. Randall W. Roth, 225-229. Honolulu: Mutual Publishing, 1993.

Odo, Franklin S. "The Japanese American Centennial in Hawaii: A Critical Look at Ethnic Celebration." *Hawaiian Journal of History*, 19 (1985), 1-16.

_____. Interview. Honolulu, November 21, 1994.

Ogawa, Dennis M. *Kodomo no tame ni (For the sake of the children): The Japanese American Experience in Hawaii*. Honolulu: University Press of Hawaii, 1978.

_____. Interview. Honolulu, March 1, 1995.

Okamura, Jonathan Y. "Aloha Kanaka Me Ke Aloha 'Aina: Local Culture and Society in Hawaii." Amerasia, 7:2 (1980), 119-137.

_____. "Beyond Adaptationism: Immigrant Filipino Ethnicity in Hawaii." *Social Process in Hawaii*, 33 (1991), 56-72.

_____. "Why There Are No Asian Americans in Hawaii: The Continuing Significance of Local Identity." *Social Process in Hawaii*, 35 (1994), 161-178.

Plasch, Bruce S. "Does Tourism Provide Mostly Low-income Jobs?" In *The Price of Paradise: Volume II*, ed. Randall W. Roth, 109-114. Honolulu: Mutual Publishing, 1993.

Phillips, Paul C. *Hawaii's Democrats: Chasing the American Dream*. Washington, DC.: University Press of America, Inc., 1982.

Phillips, Paul C. "Hawaii's Democrats: A Study of Factionalism." Unpublished Doctoral Dissertation, University of Hawaii, 1979.

Ponce, Danilo E. "The Filipinos." In *Peoples and Cultures of Hawaii: A Psychocultural Profile*, eds. John T. McDermott, Jr., Wen-shing Tseng, and Thomas W. Maretzki, 155-163. Honolulu: John A. Burns School of Medicine and The University Press of Hawaii, 1980.

Pratt, Richard C., and Zachary A. Smith, eds. *Politics and Public Policy in Hawaii*. Albany: State University of New York Press, 1992.

Puette, William J. "Media Portrayals of Organized Labor: The Limits of American Liberalism." Unpublished Doctoral Dissertation, University of Hawaii, 1989.

Pukui, Mary Kawena, and Samuel H. Elbert. *Hawaiian Dictionary*. Honolulu: University of Hawaii Press, 1986.

Pukui, Mary Kawena, Samuel H. Elbert, and Esther T. Mookini. *Place Names of Hawaii*. Honolulu: University of Hawaii Press, 1974.

Rapson, Richard L. *Fairly Lucky You Live Hawaii! Cultural Pluralism in the Fiftieth State*. Honolulu: University of Hawaii, 1980.

_____. Interview. Honolulu, February 28, 1995.

"REACH Domestic Violence Intervention Program: Resources of Emergency Assistance to Clinics & Hospitals." Unpublished brochure. Honolulu: Hawaii State Department of Human Services, 1994.

Rees, Robert M. Interview. Honolulu, March 29, 1995.

Rimonte, Nilda. "Domestic Violence Among Pacific Asians." In *Making Waves: An Anthology of Writings By and About Asian American Women*, ed. Asian Women United of California, 327-337. Boston: Beacon Press, 1989.

Roffman, Marian H. "Cultural Factors in the Union Activity of Women in Hawaii." *Social Process in Hawaii*, 28 (1980-81), 73-87.

Rogers, Terence A., and Satoru Izutsu. "The Japanese." In *Peoples and Cultures of Hawaii: A Psychocultural Profile*, eds. John T. McDermott, Jr., Wen-shing Tseng, and Thomas W. Maretzki, 73-99. Honolulu: John A. Burns School of Medicine and The University Press of Hawaii, 1980.

Rohrer, Judy. "Haole Girl: Identity and White Privilege in Hawai'i." In *Women in Hawai'i: Sites, Identities, and Voices*, eds. Joyce N. Chinen, Kathleen O. Kane and Ida M. Yoshinaga, 140-161. Honolulu: University of Hawaii Press, 1997.

Rosegg, Peter. "How Well Are We Being Represented in Washington D.C.?" In *The Price of Paradise: Volume II*, ed. Randall W. Roth, 281-287. Honolulu: Mutual Publishing, 1993.

Rosen, Sidney M. "Cec Heftel: New Politics and the Media Man." Unpublished Doctoral Dissertation, University of Hawaii, 1985.

Ross, Martha. Interview. Honolulu, May 2, 1995.

Roth, Randall W., ed. *The Price of Paradise: Lucky We Live Hawaii?* Honolulu: Mutual Publishing, 1992.

_____. *The Price of Paradise: Volume II.* Honolulu: Mutual Publishing, 1993.

Ruch, Libby O., and Susan M. Chandler. "Ethnicity and Rape Impact: The Responses of Women from Different Ethnic Backgrounds to Rape and to Rape Crisis Treatment Services in Hawaii." *Social Process in Hawaii*, 27 (1979), 52-67.

Ruch, Libby O. "Sex Roles in Hawaii: Structure and Dimensions." *Social Process in Hawaii*, 28 (1980-81), 88-97.

Russell, Anne. "Patsy Takemoto Mink: Political Woman." Unpublished Doctoral Dissertation, University of Hawaii, 1977.

Saiki, Pat. Interview. Honolulu, March 10, 1995.

Saiki, Patsy Sumie, *Japanese Women in Hawaii: The First 100 Years.* Honolulu: Kisaku, Inc., 1985.

Samuels, Frederick. *The Japanese and the Haoles of Honolulu: Durable Group Interaction.* New Haven, Connecticut: College & University Press, 1970.

Sato, Charlene J. "Linguistic Inequality in Hawaii: The Post-Creole Dilemma." In *Language of Inequality*, eds. Nessa Wolfson and Joan Manes, 255-272. Berlin: Mouton Publishers, 1985.

Schmitt, Robert C. "Hawaii's Social Rating." *Social Process in Hawaii*, 29 (1982), 151-159.

_____. Interview. Honolulu, June 22, 1995.

"Shelters of Abused Spouses and Children: Safety Advocacy Self-Empowerment Confidentiality." Unpublished brochure. Honolulu: Hawaii State Department of Human Services, 1994.

Silva, Noenoe K. "Kūʻē! Hawaiian Women's Resistance to the Annexation." In *Women in Hawaiʻi: Sites, Identities, and Voices*, eds. Joyce N. Chinen, Kathleen O. Kane and Ida M. Yoshinaga, 4-16. Honolulu: University of Hawaii Press, 1997.

Simpich, Frederick, Jr. *Anatomy of Hawaii.* Toronto: Coward, McCann & Geoghegan, 1971.

Smyser, A. A. Interview. Honolulu, March 10, 1995.

Sobin, Judy M., and Bettie Wallace. "Impact of the ERA in Hawaii." In "The Changing Lives of Hawaii's Women: Progress Since Statehood," ed. Ruth Lieben, 37. Honolulu: Foundation for Hawaii Women's History, 1985.

Soriano, Fred. "Filipino Hawaiian Migration and Adaptation: New Paradigms for Analysis." *Social Process in Hawaii*, 29 (1982), 163-179.

Spickard, Paul R. *Mixed Blood: Intermarriage and Ethnic Identity in Twentieth-Century America*. Madison: University of Wisconsin Press, 1989.

Takaki, Ronald. *Pau Hana: Plantation Life and Labor in Hawaii 1835-1920*. Honolulu: University of Hawaii Press, 1983.

Tamayose, Tremaine. "Local People: An Oral History Experiment." Honolulu: Ethnic Studies Oral History Project, University of Hawaii, 1982.

Tamura, Eileen H. *Americanization, Acculturation, and Ethnic Identity: The Nisei Generation in Hawaii*. Chicago: University of Illinois Press, 1994.

Toguchi, Charles. Interview. Honolulu, May 18, 1995.

Trask, Haunani-Kay. *From a Native Daughter: Colonialism and Sovereignty in Hawaii*. Monroe, Maine: Common Courage Press, 1993.

_____. "The Birth of the Modern Hawaiian Movement: Kalama Valley, Oahu." *Hawaiian Journal of History*, 21 (1987), 126-153.

_____. "Hawaiians, American Colonization, and the Quest for Independence." *Social Process in Hawaii*, 31 (1984), 101-136.

_____. "The Office of Hawaiian Affairs: Self-Determination or State Dependency?" *Social Process in Hawaii*, 30 (1983), 104-112.

Trimillos, Ricardo. Interview. Honolulu, April 3, 1995.

Turnbull, Phyllis, and Kathy E. Ferguson. "Military Presence/ Missionary Past: The Historical Construction of Masculine Order and Feminine Hawai'i." In *Women in Hawai'i: Sites, Identities, and Voices*, eds. Joyce N. Chinen, Kathleen O. Kane and Ida M. Yoshinaga, 96-106. Honolulu: University of Hawaii Press, 1997.

Tuttle, Daniel W., Jr., ed. "Papers of Hawaiian Politics 1952-1966." Honolulu: Hawaii State Program in Political Parties, 1966.

Tuttle, Daniel W., Jr. "A Significant Aspect of the 1964 Hawaii Election: The personality Campaign of United States Senator Hiram L. Fong." In "Papers of Hawaiian Politics 1952-1966," ed. Daniel W. Tuttle, Jr., 135-139. Honolulu: Hawaii State Program in Political Parties, 1966.

_____. "1976 Hawaii Voting Behavior: A Background Guide to Some Significant Characteristics of Hawaii's 234 Precincts." Honolulu: Public Affairs Advisory Services, Inc., 1978.

_____. Interview. Honolulu, April 25, 1995.

U.S. Department of Interior. "Hawaii and Its Race Problem." New York: AMS Press, 1979.

Wang, James C.F. Hawaii State and Local Politics. Hilo, Hawaii: J.C.F. Wang, 1982.

Ward Research, "Viewership of Voter Information Program: A Survey of Cable Television Subscribers Executive Summary." Unpublished manuscript prepared for Olelo, the Corporation for Community Television. Honolulu: November 1994.

Wernet, Bob. Interview. Honolulu, November 12, 1994.

West Hawaii Today. Kona, Hawaii: September and November 1994.

Whittaker, Elvi. The Mainland Haole: The White Experience in Hawaii. New York: Columbia University Press, 1986.

Wittermans, Elizabeth. "Inter-Ethnic Relations in Hawaii." Social Process in Hawaii, 28 (1980-81), 148-161.

Wooden, Wayne S. What Price Paradise? Changing Social Patterns in Hawaii. Washington, D.C.: University Press of America, 1981.

Wright, Paul. "Ethnic Differences in the Outmigration of Local-Born Residents from Hawaii." Social Process in Hawaii, 30 (1983), 7-31.

Wright, Theon. The Disenchanted Isles: The Story of the Second Revolution in Hawaii. New York: Dial Press, 1972.

Yamamoto, Eric. "The Significance of Local." Social Process in Hawaii, 27 (1979), 101-115.

Yamamura, Douglas S., and Harry V. Ball. "Hawaii's People and Lifestyles 2000." In Hawaii 2000: Continuing Experiment in Anticipatory Democracy, eds. George Chaplin and Glenn D. Paige, 141-161. Honolulu: University Press of Hawaii, 1973.

Yang, Sarah Lee. "Koreans in Hawaii." Social Process in Hawaii, 29 (1982), 89-94.

Young, Benjamin B.C. "The Hawaiians." In Peoples and Cultures of Hawaii: A Psychocultural Profile, eds. John T. McDermott, Jr., Wenshing Tseng, and Thomas W. Maretzki, 5-24. Honolulu: John A. Burns School of Medicine and The University Press of Hawaii, 1980.

Young, Jackie. Interview. Honolulu, June 1, 1995.

Young, Nancy Foo, and Judy R. Parrish, eds. "Montage: An Ethnic History of Women in Hawaii." Honolulu: General Assistance Center for the Pacific, College of Education, Educational Foundation, University of Hawaii, and State Commission on the Status of Women, 1977.

Yount, David. Who Runs the University? Honolulu: University of Hawaii Press, 1996.

INDEX

ABOUT THE AUTHOR

Chad Blair earned a Ph.D. in American Studies from the University of Hawaiʻi at Mānoa. A self-avowed "political junkie," he teaches political science at Hawaiʻi Pacific University and American culture and English at Hawaiʻi Tokai International College. His writings have appeared in various Hawaiʻi publications.